MEDITERRANEAN COOKING

FOR BEGINNERS!

Delicious recipes for a
Mediterranean diet lifestyle

Publications International, Ltd.

ISBN: 978-1-64030-820-6

Manufactured in China.

8 7 6 5 4 3 2 1

Let's get social!

@Publications_International

@PublicationsInternational

www.pilcookbooks.com

CONTENTS

WHAT IS THE MEDITERRANEAN DIET?

Let's start with what it isn't. It is not an extreme elimination plan, a calorie- or carbohydrate-counting plan or an unrealistically restrictive plan. It is a mostly common-sense approach to eating modeled on the eating habits of countries that border the Mediterranean Sea. These include European countries: Spain, France, Italy and Greece; Middle Eastern countries: Turkey, Syria and Lebanon; and African countries: Egypt, Libya, Tunisia, Algeria and Morocco.

This diverse list of countries may not seem to have much in common at first, but as you examine the native cuisines of the people, a pattern emerges: an emphasis on fresh vegetables, fruit, whole grains, fish and seafood, healthy unsaturated fats, and smaller amounts of meat, dairy and refined grains. There is a lifestyle component as well, a mindful approach to meals. Minimize distractions (phones, television, etc.), focusing instead on eating slowly and enjoying every bite.

HOW DO I EAT MEDITERRANEAN?

The Mediterranean diet is primarily plant based, so plan on basing your meals on vegetables, fruit, grains and legumes with a bit of dairy thrown in for seasoning. Add fish, seafood or chicken a few times a week, and reserve red meat for occasional (once a week) treats. If reducing the amount of meat in your diet seems too difficult, start small and try one or two nights a week without it. As you can see from the Mediterranean food pyramid, there are plenty of delicious options.

A perfect example of this is Mujadara on page 112. It is a staple dish of Lebanese cuisine consisting of lentils, rice and onions, and is delicious accompanied by a cucumber-yogurt sauce. It is hearty, filling and packed with grains and legumes. You can build on it by adding pita bread (page 156) and/or a Greek salad (page 50), all of which happen to make great leftovers for lunch or as a part of a mezze selection (see page 6).

TIPS FOR GETTING STARTED AND STAYING ON TRACK

- **Get organized.** Clean out your pantry and get rid of unhealthy snacks like chips, cookies, candy and replace them with better choices like roasted nuts, olives, fresh fruit like grapes, apples and oranges. Plan your meals in advance, and try to pick things that have similar ingredients. It's easier to buy larger quantities fewer items than it is to buy small quantities of more items. Also, it will help you stay focused and give you less to think about if you know that you're using, say, tomatoes, cucumbers, onions for several meals rather than different ingredients every night.

MONTHLY
OR SMALL AMOUNTS

MEATS
SWEETS

DAILY TO WEEKLY

EGGS, CHEESE,
POULTRY, YOGURT

A FEW TIMES PER WEEK

FISH, SEAFOOD

IN VARIABLE AMOUNTS

OLIVE OIL

DAILY SERVINGS

FRUITS,
VEGETABLES

DAILY SERVINGS

WHOLE GRAINS,
BREAD, BEANS,
PASTA, NUTS

DAILY PHYSICAL ACTIVITY

MEDITERRANEAN DIET

- **Spend some time each week cleaning out your refrigerator.** Discard any leftovers that are long past their prime, and plan a night to serve recent leftovers as a mezze spread. Check the status of your eggs, Greek yogurt, feta cheese and cucumbers and keep a running list of what's running low.

- **As long as you're making good food decisions, make good beverage choices as well.** Instead of sugary sodas and coffee drinks, try tea and coffee either black or with a splash of cream and a drizzle of honey (yes, even in coffee—it's good!). Instead of soda, try plain sparkling water mixed with a squeeze of fresh lime, lemon or grapefruit juice. Or infuse regular water with cucumber, mint and/or lemon; keep a pitcher in your refrigerator or stick a mint sprig and a lemon wedge in your water bottle for flavored water throughout the day.

MEZZE

Mezze is a style of dining where small plates make up a meal, similar to tapas.

Pick a recipe from the Small Plates chapter like Mediterranean Baked Feta (page 30) or Classic Hummus (page 32), a recipe from the Salads and Vegetables chapter like Greek Salad (page 50) or House Salad (page 62), perhaps, and a cooked dish like Feta Frittata (page 7) or Spiced Chicken Skewers with Yogurt-Tahini Sauce (page 118).

Or give it a try at the end of the week when you've got little bits of leftovers to use up—just buy or make some fresh pita, whip up a fresh salad and set out cold salads, grain dishes and meats leftover from the week.

- **Keep rice, lentils, pasta, nuts and cheese on hand.** Not only will you need them to make many Mediterranean recipes, but they're great to have on hand for simple last-minute meals. Marinated Feta (see sidebar) is great to have on hand for snacking or adding to salads or pasta dishes. Instead of resorting to takeout or junk food, try a simple dinner using pantry staples. Try Risi Bisi (page 97), Lentils with Walnuts (page 108), Pasta with Onions and Goat Cheese (page 92) or one of the following suggestions.

AGLIO E OLIO: Cook 8 ounces of pasta in boiling salted water until al dente. Meanwhile, heat $1/4$ cup olive oil in large skillet over medium heat. Add 4 cloves garlic, thinly sliced, and cook just until garlic begins to brown on edges. Season with $1/2$ teaspoon salt and some red pepper flakes. Add some fresh bread crumbs, if desired (process bread in the food processor, or finely chop with a knife); cook and stir until golden. Add the hot pasta to the skillet, tossing to coat with oil. Serve topped with chopped fresh parsley and shredded Parmesan cheese, if desired.

NO-COOK TOMATO SAUCE: Core, seed and dice fresh tomatoes to equal about 4 cups. Add $1/4$ cup olive oil, 2 minced garlic cloves and a small handful of shredded fresh basil or parsley, if desired. Season with salt and pepper to taste. Add some cubed fresh mozzarella, feta or chunks of Brie cheese, if desired. Let stand at room temperature while you cook 8 to 12 ounces of pasta in boiling salted water until al dente. Drain pasta and toss with tomato mixture until coated.

A FRITTATA WITH ANYTHING: Start with the recipe for the Feta Frittata on page 7. If you've got leftover pasta, couscous, rice, lentils or meat (on their own or from a recipe), stir in $1/2$ cup to 1 cup with the eggs in step 1. Cook as directed, using the feta and pine nuts if you want, or skip them. If you've got some vegetables to use up like mushrooms, bell peppers, onions, tomatoes, zucchini or yellow squash, sauté them in the olive oil in the skillet before adding the egg mixture. Cook as directed. Top with any cheese or nuts you have (shredded Parmesan, Romano, Asiago, crumbled goat cheese, walnuts, pistachios, slivered almonds) or leave the top plain.

SCRAMBLED EGGS WITH GREEK YOGURT: Try them for any meal. They're quick, easy and delicious and make a delicious meal with toast and fruit. They're also a great accompaniment to leftover grain or bean dishes with or without a bit of meat. For each serving, whisk 2 eggs, 1 tablespoon plain Greek yogurt, 1/4 teaspoon salt and a sprinkle of black pepper in a medium bowl until well blended. Heat a small nonstick skillet over medium-high heat. Add 1 teaspoon olive oil; tilt to coat skillet. Add eggs; cook until edge begins to turn opaque. Slide silicone spatula around the edge to loosen eggs. Continue stirring in this way until eggs form large curds. Cook and stir until eggs are set and no wet spots remain (about 1 minute total). If you're making more than one serving, use a larger skillet and additional oil to coat the bottom in a thin layer.

- **Keep two kinds of olive oil on hand.** Select a decent olive oil for sautéeing and cooking and a high-quality extra virgin olive oil for making dressings and sauces and using in other places where you'll really taste the flavor (like the olive oil cake on page 176).

- **Try to make every meal an occasion; eating should be an enjoyable experience that is a real part of your day, not just a task to be endured.** Turn off distractions like televisions, phones and tablets, and turn on music instead. Allow enough time that everyone can eat at their own pace without feeling rushed. If you need to train yourself to eat slower, put down your fork after every bite, and chew and swallow before picking it up again.

MARINATED FETA

1 pound (16 ounces) feta cheese, cubed

1/2 cup extra virgin olive oil

2 tablespoons finely minced green bell pepper

2 tablespoons finely minced red bell pepper

2 to 3 cloves garlic, finely minced

1 tablespoon chopped fresh Italian parsley *or* 1 teaspoon dried parsley flakes

2 teaspoons fresh rosemary leaves *or* 1 teaspoon dried rosemary

1 teaspoon peppercorns

1/2 teaspoon *each* salt, black pepper and red pepper flakes

Place all ingredients in clean, dry, large glass jar with tight-fitting lid. Marinate in refrigerator several hours or up to several days. Flip jar upside-down occasionally to immerse cheese in seasonings and oil. Serve with toasted baguette slices, crackers, fruit or vegetables, if desired. As cheese is used up, additional cubed cheese can be added to jar, or remaining herb-oil mixture can be made into vinaigrette dressing by adding vinegar to the jar. Shake jar before serving.

BREAKFAST

FETA FRITTATA

MAKES 4 SERVINGS

1. Preheat broiler. Whisk eggs, yogurt, basil, salt and pepper in medium bowl until well blended.

2. Heat oil in large ovenproof skillet over medium heat, tilting skillet to coat bottom and side. Pour egg mixture into skillet; cover and cook 8 to 10 minutes or until eggs are set around edge (center will be wet).

3. Sprinkle feta and pine nuts evenly over top. Transfer to broiler; broil 4 to 5 inches from heat source 2 minutes or until center is set and pine nuts are golden brown. Cut into wedges.

TIP: This frittata also makes a great meal. Cut it into quarters and serve it hot with fruit for breakfast, tuck a wedge into half a pita for lunch, or serve it alongside Parmesan Potato Wedges (page 52) for dinner.

- 8 eggs
- ¼ cup plain Greek yogurt
- ¼ cup chopped fresh basil
- ½ teaspoon salt
- ¼ teaspoon black pepper
- 1 tablespoon olive oil
- 1 package (4 ounces) crumbled feta cheese with basil, olives and sun-dried tomatoes *or* 1 cup crumbled plain feta cheese
- ¼ cup pine nuts

FIG-ALMOND OATMEAL

MAKES 6 SERVINGS

1. Bring water to a boil in large saucepan over high heat. Stir in oats, figs, almonds, brown sugar, flax seeds, salt and cinnamon. Immediately add 2 cups milk. Stir well.

2. Reduce heat to medium-high. Cook and stir 5 to 7 minutes or until oatmeal is thick and creamy. Spoon into serving bowls. Serve with additional milk, if desired.

TIP: Oatmeal is a great make-ahead breakfast. Divide servings among microwavable glass jars or storage containers and refrigerate. Uncover and microwave until heated through, adding additional milk or water to thin to desired consistency.

2 cups water

2¾ cups old-fashioned oats

½ cup finely diced dried figs

½ cup sliced almonds, toasted*

⅓ cup lightly packed dark brown sugar or honey

¼ cup flax seeds

½ teaspoon salt

½ teaspoon ground cinnamon

2 cups milk, plus additional for serving

To toast almonds, spread in single layer in heavy skillet. Cook over medium heat 2 to 3 minutes or until lightly browned, stirring frequently.

BUCKWHEAT PANCAKES

MAKES 12 PANCAKES

1. Whisk buckwheat flour, cornstarch, baking powder, salt and cinnamon in medium bowl. Whisk milk, egg, 2 tablespoons oil, 2 tablespoons maple syrup and vanilla in small bowl. Gradually whisk into dry ingredients just until combined. Let stand 5 minutes. (Batter will be thick and elastic.)

2. Brush griddle or large nonstick skillet with additional oil; heat over medium heat. Pour ¼ cupfuls of batter 2 inches apart onto griddle. Cook 2 minutes or until lightly browned and edges begin to bubble. Turn and cook 2 minutes or until lightly browned. Serve with additional maple syrup.

VARIATION: Add ½ cup blueberries to the batter.

- 1 cup buckwheat flour
- 2 tablespoons cornstarch
- 2 teaspoons baking powder
- ¼ teaspoon salt
- ¼ teaspoon ground cinnamon
- 1 cup whole milk
- 1 egg
- 2 tablespoons grapeseed oil or olive oil, plus additional for cooking
- 2 tablespoons maple syrup, plus additional for serving
- ½ teaspoon vanilla

SPINACH, MUSHROOM AND EGG ROLLUPS

MAKES 4 SERVINGS

1. Heat 2 teaspoons oil in large nonstick skillet over medium heat. Add shallot; cook and stir 5 to 6 minutes until softened. Increase heat to medium-high. Add spinach; cook 2 minutes until wilted. Add garlic and $\frac{1}{4}$ teaspoon salt; cook and stir 30 seconds. Transfer to small bowl.

2. Heat 1 tablespoon oil in same skillet over medium-high heat. Add mushrooms, $\frac{1}{2}$ teaspoon salt and $\frac{1}{8}$ teaspoon pepper; cook 6 minutes or until browned, stirring occasionally. Stir in spinach mixture; remove from heat.

3. Spread mushroom mixture on flatbreads; sprinkle evenly with cheese.

4. Whisk eggs, milk, mustard, remaining $\frac{1}{4}$ teaspoon salt and $\frac{1}{8}$ teaspoon pepper in large bowl.

5. Heat remaining 2 teaspoons oil in same skillet over medium-high heat. Add egg mixture; cook about 1 minute, stirring frequently, until eggs are set but not dry.

6. Place cooked eggs on mushroom mixture; roll up flatbreads. Cut in half to serve.

MAKE AHEAD: Prepare rollups ahead of time and reheat in microwave when ready to eat.

1 tablespoon plus 4 teaspoons olive oil, divided

1 shallot, thinly sliced (about $\frac{1}{2}$ cup)

1 bag (6 ounces) fresh baby spinach

1 clove garlic, minced

1 teaspoon salt, divided

8 ounces cremini mushrooms, thinly sliced

$\frac{1}{4}$ teaspoon black pepper, divided

2 pieces flatbread (such as naan, about 9×11-inches), lightly toasted

$\frac{2}{3}$ cup shredded Grùyere cheese

6 eggs

2 tablespoons milk

2 teaspoons Dijon mustard

BUCKWHEAT BREAKFAST BOWL

MAKES 6 SERVINGS

1. Combine milk, brown sugar, salt, vanilla and ¼ teaspoon cinnamon in large saucepan. Bring to a boil over medium heat. Stir in kasha; reduce heat to low. Cook and stir 8 to 10 minutes or until kasha is tender and liquid is absorbed.

2. Meanwhile, cut apples into ribbons with thick spiral blade of spiralizer; coarsely chop to shorten long pieces.*** Melt butter in large nonstick skillet over medium heat. Stir in remaining ¼ teaspoon cinnamon. Add apples; cook and stir 4 to 5 minutes or until tender. Stir in maple syrup and walnuts; heat through.

3. Spoon kasha into six bowls. Top with apple mixture. Serve immediately.

***Or cut apples into matchsticks or finely dice.*

3 to 4 cups milk*

2 tablespoons packed brown sugar

½ teaspoon salt

½ teaspoon vanilla

½ teaspoon ground cinnamon, divided

1 cup kasha**

2 apples

2 teaspoons butter

2 tablespoons maple syrup

¼ cup chopped walnuts

For a creamier consistency, use more milk.

**Kasha, or buckwheat groats, is buckwheat that has been pre-toasted. It is commonly found in the Kosher section of the supermarket.*

ASPARAGUS FRITTATA PROSCIUTTO CUPS

MAKES 12 CUPS (6 SERVINGS)

1. Preheat oven to 375°F. Spray 12 standard (2¹/₂-inch) muffin cups with nonstick cooking spray.

2. Heat oil in large skillet over medium heat. Add onion; cook and stir 4 minutes or until softened. Add asparagus and garlic; cook and stir 8 minutes or until asparagus is crisp-tender. Set aside to cool slightly.

3. Line each prepared muffin cup with prosciutto slice. (Prosciutto should cover cup as much as possible, with edges extending above muffin pan.) Whisk eggs, Cheddar, Parmesan, milk and pepper in large bowl until well blended. Stir in asparagus mixture until blended. Pour into prosciutto-lined cups, filling about three-fourths full.

4. Bake about 20 minutes or until frittatas are puffed and golden brown and edges are pulling away from pan. Cool in pan 10 minutes; remove to wire rack. Serve warm or at room temperature.

- 1 tablespoon olive oil
- 1 small red onion, finely chopped
- 1¹/₂ cups sliced asparagus (¹/₂-inch pieces)
- 1 clove garlic, minced
- 12 thin slices prosciutto
- 8 eggs
- ¹/₂ cup (2 ounces) grated white Cheddar cheese
- ¹/₄ cup grated Parmesan cheese
- 2 tablespoons milk
- ¹/₈ teaspoon black pepper

QUINOA AND OAT MUESLI

MAKES ABOUT 7 CUPS

1. Preheat oven to 350°F. Spread quinoa in single layer on baking sheet. Bake 8 to 10 minutes until toasted and golden brown, stirring frequently. (Quinoa will make a slight popping sound when almost done.) Remove from oven. Transfer quinoa to small bowl; cool completely.

2. Combine oats, coconut, almonds and cinnamon in large bowl. Spread in even layer on same baking sheet. Bake 15 minutes or until mixture is lightly toasted and fragrant, stirring once. Cool completely on baking sheet.

3. Combine cooled quinoa and oat mixture in large bowl; add wheat germ, flaxseed and dried fruit. Stir to combine.

4. Serve with yogurt, fresh fruit and honey.

- 1 cup uncooked quinoa
- 3 cups old-fashioned rolled oats
- 1/4 cup unsweetened flaked coconut
- 3/4 cup coarsely chopped almonds
- 1/2 teaspoon ground cinnamon
- 1/2 cup toasted wheat germ
- 1/4 cup ground flaxseed
- 1 1/4 cups dried or freeze-dried fruit

  Plain Greek yogurt, cut-up fresh fruit and honey for serving

PEPPER AND EGG COUSCOUS BOWL

MAKES 4 SERVINGS

1. Heat oil in large skillet over medium-high heat. Add bell peppers and onion; cook and stir 5 minutes or until vegetables are tender.

2. Bring broth to a boil in small saucepan. Stir in couscous, garlic, salt, oregano and cumin. Remove from heat. Cover and let stand 5 minutes. Fluff with fork.

3. Serve vegetables, beans and eggs over couscous; top with tomatoes and cheese, if desired.

1 tablespoon olive oil

3 bell peppers, assorted colors, thinly sliced

1 red onion, halved and thinly sliced

2 cups vegetable broth

1 cup uncooked couscous

1 clove garlic, minced

1/2 teaspoon salt

1/2 teaspoon dried oregano

1/2 teaspoon ground cumin

1 can (15 ounces) black beans or black-eyed peas, rinsed and drained

4 to 8 eggs, cooked any style

1 cup grape tomatoes, halved

Crumbled feta cheese (optional)

TOMATO-PROSCIUTTO FRITTATA

MAKES 4 TO 6 SERVINGS

1. Heat ¼ cup oil in large skillet over medium-high heat. Add onions; cook and stir 8 to 10 minutes until soft and golden. Reduce heat to medium. Add tomatoes; cook 5 minutes. Transfer vegetables to large bowl with slotted spoon; discard drippings. Cool to room temperature.

2. Stir prosciutto, Parmesan, parsley, marjoram, salt, basil and pepper into onion mixture. Whisk eggs in medium bowl until well blended; stir into prosciutto mixture.

3. Preheat broiler. Heat remaining 2 tablespoons oil in medium broilerproof skillet over medium heat. Reduce heat to low; add egg mixture. Cook 8 to 10 minutes until edge is set but center is still soft. (Shake pan gently to test.) *Do not stir.*

4. Broil frittata about 4 inches from heat 1 to 2 minutes or until top is set. (Do not brown or frittata will be dry.) Serve warm or at room temperature. Cut into wedges.

- ¼ cup plus 2 tablespoons olive oil, divided
- 5 small onions, thinly sliced
- 1 can (about 14 ounces) whole peeled tomatoes, drained and chopped
- 4 ounces prosciutto or cooked ham, chopped
- ¼ cup grated Parmesan cheese
- 2 tablespoons chopped fresh parsley
- ½ teaspoon dried marjoram
- ¼ teaspoon salt
- ¼ teaspoon dried basil
- ⅛ teaspoon black pepper
- 6 eggs

SMALL PLATES

KASHK-E BADEMJAN (PERSIAN EGGPLANT DIP)

MAKES 12 TO 16 SERVINGS

1. Toss eggplant with salt in large bowl; transfer to large colander. Place colander in large bowl or sink; let stand 1 hour at room temperature to drain.

2. Meanwhile, heat 1 tablespoon oil in large nonstick skillet over medium-high heat. Add onions; cook 5 to 6 minutes or until lightly browned, stirring occasionally. Transfer to slow cooker. Stir in eggplant. Cover; cook on LOW 6 to 8 hours or on HIGH 3½ to 4 hours or until eggplant is very soft.

3. Heat remaining 4 tablespoons oil in small saucepan over low heat. Add mint; cook about 15 minutes or until very fragrant. Set aside to cool slightly.

4. Transfer eggplant and onions to colander or fine mesh strainer with slotted spoon; press out any excess liquid with back of spoon. Return to slow cooker; mash with fork. Stir in yogurt. Sprinkle with chopped walnuts; drizzle with mint oil. Serve warm with pita bread and/or assorted vegetable sticks.

3 large eggplants (3½ pounds total), peeled and cut into 1-inch cubes

1 teaspoon salt

5 tablespoons olive oil, divided

2 onions, chopped

1 tablespoon dried mint

3 tablespoons plain Greek yogurt

⅓ cup finely chopped walnuts

Pita bread and/or assorted vegetable sticks

SPANAKOPITA

MAKES 4 TO 8 SERVINGS

1. Preheat oven to 375°F. Spray 8-inch square baking pan with nonstick cooking spray.

2. Heat 1 teaspoon oil in large skillet over medium heat. Add onion; cook and stir 5 to 6 minutes or until soft. Add garlic; cook and stir 30 seconds. Add spinach and cheese; cook and stir until spinach is heated through. Remove from heat.

3. Place 1 sheet of phyllo dough on counter with long side toward you. (Cover remaining sheets with damp towel until needed.) Brush right half of phyllo with oil; fold left half over. Place sheet in prepared pan. (Two edges will hang over sides of pan.) Brush top of sheet with oil. Brush and fold 2 more sheets of phyllo the same way. Place sheets in pan at 90° angles so edges will hang over all 4 sides of pan. Brush each sheet with oil after it is placed in pan.

4. Whisk eggs, salt, nutmeg and pepper in small bowl. Stir into spinach mixture until blended. Spread filling over phyllo in pan. Brush and fold 1 sheet phyllo as above; place on top of filling, tucking ends under filling. Bring all overhanging edges of phyllo over top sheet; brush lightly with oil. Brush and fold last sheet as above; place over top sheet, tucking ends under. Brush lightly with oil.

5. Bake 25 to 27 minutes or until top is barely browned. Cool 10 to 15 minutes. Cut into quarters, strips or wedges before serving.

Olive oil

1 **large onion, thinly sliced**

2 **cloves garlic, minced**

1 **package (10 ounces) frozen chopped spinach, thawed and squeezed dry**

1/2 **cup crumbled feta cheese**

5 **sheets phyllo dough, thawed***

2 **eggs**

1/2 **teaspoon salt**

1/4 **teaspoon ground nutmeg**

1/8 **teaspoon black pepper**

*Thaw entire package of phyllo dough overnight in refrigerator.

MEDITERRANEAN BAKED FETA

MAKES 4 TO 6 SERVINGS

1. Preheat oven to 400°F.

2. Place cheese in small baking dish; top with tomatoes, roasted peppers and olives. Sprinkle with oregano and season with black pepper; drizzle with oil.

3. Bake 12 minutes or until cheese is soft. Sprinkle with basil. Serve immediately with pita chips.

1 package (8 ounces) feta cheese, cut crosswise into 4 slices

$1/2$ cup grape tomatoes, halved

$1/4$ cup sliced roasted peppers

$1/4$ cup pitted kalamata olives

$1/8$ teaspoon dried oregano

Black pepper

2 tablespoons extra virgin olive oil

1 tablespoon shredded fresh basil

Pita chips, store-bought or homemade (page 155)

CLASSIC HUMMUS ▶
MAKES ABOUT 2½ CUPS

1. Combine chickpeas, tahini, lemon juice, garlic and salt in food processor; process until blended. With motor running, add ice water in thin steady stream. Process 5 minutes until hummus is fluffy and very smooth.

2. Spread in serving bowl; drizzle with oil and sprinkle with paprika, if desired. Store leftovers in jar or other airtight container in the refrigerator for 3 days.

- 1 can (30 ounces) chickpeas, drained
- 1 cup tahini
- ¼ cup fresh lemon juice
- 1 clove garlic
- 1 teaspoon salt
- ¼ cup ice water
- Extra virgin olive oil and paprika

PAPRIKA ALMONDS
MAKES ABOUT 8 SERVINGS

1. Preheat oven to 375°F. Spread almonds in single layer in shallow baking pan. Bake 8 to 10 minutes or until almonds are lightly browned. Transfer to bowl; cool 5 to 10 minutes.

2. Toss almonds with oil until completely coated. Sprinkle with salt and paprika; toss again.

TIP: For the best flavor, serve these almonds the day they are made.

- 1 cup whole blanched almonds
- 1 teaspoon olive oil
- ½ teaspoon coarse salt
- ¼ teaspoon smoked or sweet paprika

CAPER-RICE CROQUETTES

MAKES 6 SERVINGS

1. Bring water to a boil in small saucepan over high heat. Stir in rice. Reduce heat to low; cover and simmer about 14 minutes or until rice is tender and water is absorbed. Transfer rice to medium bowl; cool until almost room temperature.

2. Add prosciutto, egg yolk, capers, salt, oregano and pepper; mix well. Spread bread crumbs on large plate. Shape rice mixture into 18 ($1\frac{1}{4}$-inch) balls. Flatten slightly; carefully coat with bread crumbs. Place on plate; refrigerate 15 to 30 minutes until firm.

3. Heat oil in heavy medium skillet over medium-high heat. Add half of croquettes; cook 2 to 3 minutes or until golden brown. Turn and cook 1 to 2 minutes or until golden brown. Transfer to plate; keep warm. Repeat with remaining croquettes, adding additional oil if necessary. Serve hot.

$2/3$ cup water

$1/3$ cup uncooked long or medium grain white rice

2 ounces prosciutto, finely chopped

1 egg yolk

1 tablespoon capers, drained and rinsed

$1/4$ teaspoon salt

$1/8$ teaspoon dried oregano

$1/8$ teaspoon black pepper

$2/3$ cup fresh bread crumbs

2 tablespoons olive oil

ASPARAGUS AND PROSCIUTTO ANTIPASTO ▶

MAKES 12 APPETIZERS

1. Trim and discard tough ends of asparagus spears. Simmer asparagus in salted water in large skillet 4 to 5 minutes or until crisp-tender. Drain and rinse under cold water until cool. Pat dry with paper towels.

2. Combine cream cheese, blue cheese and pepper in small bowl; mix well. Cut prosciutto slices in half crosswise to make 12 pieces. Spread cream cheese mixture evenly over one side of each prosciutto slice. Wrap around asparagus. Serve at room temperature or slightly chilled.

12 asparagus spears (about 8 ounces)

2 ounces cream cheese, softened

$\frac{1}{4}$ cup crumbled blue cheese or goat cheese

$\frac{1}{4}$ teaspoon black pepper

1 package (3 to 4 ounces) thinly sliced prosciutto

TOMATO AND CAPER CROSTINI

MAKES 8 CROSTINI

1. Preheat oven to 350°F.

2. Place bread slices in single layer on ungreased baking sheet. Bake 15 minutes or until golden brown. Cool completely.

3. Meanwhile, combine tomatoes, capers, basil and oil in small bowl; mix well. Season with salt and pepper. Just before serving, spoon about 1 tablespoon tomato mixture on each bread slice; sprinkle with cheese.

1 French roll, cut into 8 slices

2 plum tomatoes, finely chopped

$1\frac{1}{2}$ tablespoons capers, drained

$1\frac{1}{2}$ teaspoons dried basil

1 teaspoon extra virgin olive oil

Salt and black pepper

$\frac{1}{4}$ cup crumbled feta cheese

FALAFEL WITH GARLIC TAHINI SAUCE

MAKES 8 SERVINGS

1. Combine chickpeas and 1 teaspoon salt in large bowl. Add water to cover by at least 3 inches. Let stand 8 hours or overnight. Prepare garlic tahini sauce; refrigerate until ready to serve.

2. Drain chickpeas and transfer to food processor. Add onion, parsley, lemon juice, garlic, cumin, coriander, red pepper flakes and remaining 1 teaspoon salt. Pulse until mixture is smooth, scraping side of bowl frequently. If mixture is too dry, add 1 to 2 tablespoons water.

3. Line baking sheet with waxed paper. Shape heaping tablespoons of mixture into 1½-inch balls with dampened hands. Place on prepared baking sheet.

4. Pour oil into deep heavy saucepan to depth of 2 inches. Heat over medium-high heat to 350°F. Fry falafel in batches 3 to 5 minutes or until golden brown. Remove with slotted spoon and drain on paper towels.

5. Serve with garlic tahini sauce, pita bread and desired vegetables.

1½ cup dried chickpeas, sorted and rinsed

2 teaspoons salt, divided

Garlic Tahini Sauce (recipe follows)

1 small onion, chopped

½ cup chopped fresh parsley

1 tablespoon lemon juice

2 cloves garlic

2 teaspoons ground cumin

1 teaspoon ground coriander

½ teaspoon ground red pepper

Grapeseed or vegetable oil

Pita bread, lettuce, tomatoes, chopped cucumbers (optional)

GARLIC TAHINI SAUCE
MAKES ABOUT 1 CUP

Whisk yogurt, tahini, water, lemon juice, garlic and cumin in small bowl until well blended. Season to taste with salt. Cover; refrigerate 1 hour.

½ cup plain yogurt

¼ cup tahini

3 tablespoons cold water

2 tablespoons fresh lemon juice

1 clove garlic, minced

½ teaspoon ground cumin

Salt

BEANS AND GREENS CROSTINI

MAKES ABOUT 24 CROSTINI

1. Heat 1 tablespoon oil in large skillet over medium heat. Add onion; cook and stir 5 minutes or until softened. Add kale and 1 tablespoon garlic; cook 15 minutes or until kale is softened and most liquid has evaporated, stirring occasionally. Stir in vinegar, 1 teaspoon salt and red pepper flakes.

2. Meanwhile, combine beans, remaining 3 tablespoons oil, 1 tablespoon garlic, 1 teaspoon salt and rosemary in food processor or blender; process until smooth.

3. Spread baguette slices with bean mixture; top with kale mixture.

4 tablespoons olive oil, divided

1 small onion, thinly sliced

4 cups thinly sliced Italian black kale or other dinosaur kale variety

2 tablespoons minced garlic, divided

1 tablespoon balsamic vinegar

2 teaspoons salt, divided

1/4 teaspoon red pepper flakes

1 can (about 15 ounces) cannellini beans, rinsed and drained

1 tablespoon chopped fresh rosemary

Toasted baguette slices

TZATZIKI DIP WITH CRUDITÉS

MAKES 10 SERVINGS

1. Wrap cucumber in clean dish towel or paper towels; twist towel to squeeze juice from cucumber.

2. Place cucumber in medium bowl. Add yogurt, lemon peel, lemon juice, mint, oil, salt, garlic and vinegar; mix well. Cover and refrigerate at least 2 hours.

3. Place dip in serving bowl. Serve with vegetables.

1 cup peeled, seeded diced cucumber

2 cups plain Greek yogurt

Grated peel of 1 lemon

3 tablespoons fresh lemon juice

2 tablespoons minced fresh mint

2 tablespoons extra virgin olive oil

2 teaspoons salt

2 teaspoons minced garlic

1$\frac{1}{2}$ teaspoons white wine vinegar

Crudités: carrot sticks, zucchini sticks, bell pepper strips, trimmed green onions and grape tomatoes

ROSEMARY-LEMON PORK KABOBS

MAKES 4 SERVINGS

1. Preheat broiler.

2. Steam potatoes 6 minutes or until crisp-tender. Rinse under cold water; dry with paper towels.

3. Thread potatoes onto 4 (10-inch) metal skewers, alternating with pork and onion. Brush lightly with oil; sprinkle with rosemary and paprika and season with salt and black pepper.

4. Place kabobs on baking sheet; broil 4 minutes. Turn over; broil 4 minutes more or until pork is barely pink in center.

5. Meanwhile for glaze, whisk lemon juice, 1 tablespoon oil, lemon peel, garlic, $1/2$ teaspoon salt and $1/8$ teaspoon black pepper. Spoon lemon mixture evenly over kabobs; serve additional glaze for dipping.

TIP: For an artful presentation, serve the pork, potatoes and onion on rosemary sprigs. Broil the skewers as directed, then remove the food and thread it onto short rosemary sprigs.

KABOBS

- 4 small red potatoes, quartered
- 1 pork tenderloin (about 1 pound), cut into 16 (1-inch) cubes
- 1 small red onion, quartered and layers separated
- Olive oil
- $1/2$ teaspoon dried rosemary
- Dash paprika
- Salt and black pepper

GLAZE

- 2 tablespoons lemon juice
- 1 tablespoon olive oil
- 1 teaspoon grated lemon peel
- $1/2$ clove garlic, minced
- $1/2$ teaspoon salt
- $1/8$ teaspoon black pepper

SALADS & VEGETABLES

MEDITERRANEAN-STYLE ROASTED VEGETABLES

MAKES 6 SERVINGS

1. Preheat oven to 425°F. Spray large roasting pan with nonstick cooking spray.

2. Place potatoes in prepared pan. Drizzle with 2 tablespoons oil; toss to coat evenly. Roast 10 minutes.

3. Add bell peppers and onion to pan. Drizzle with remaining 1½ teaspoons oil. Sprinkle with garlic, salt and black pepper; toss to coat evenly.

4. Roast 18 to 20 minutes or until vegetables are browned and tender, stirring once.

5. Transfer vegetables to large serving dish. Drizzle with vinegar; toss to coat evenly. Add basil; toss again. Serve warm or at room temperature.

1½ pounds red potatoes, cut into ½-inch chunks

2 tablespoons plus 1½ teaspoons olive oil, divided

1 red bell pepper, cut into ½-inch pieces

1 yellow or orange bell pepper, cut into ½-inch pieces

1 small red onion, cut into ½-inch wedges

2 cloves garlic, minced

½ teaspoon salt

¼ teaspoon black pepper

1 tablespoon balsamic vinegar

¼ cup chopped fresh basil

SPANISH TAPAS POTATOES (PATATAS BRAVAS)

MAKES 10 TO 12 SERVINGS

1. Preheat oven to 425°F.

2. Combine potatoes, 2 tablespoons oil, coarse salt and rosemary in large bowl; toss to coat. Spread mixture in large shallow baking pan. Roast potatoes 35 to 40 minutes or until crisp and brown, turning every 10 minutes.

3. For sauce, combine tomatoes, remaining $1/3$ cup oil, vinegar, garlic, chili powder, paprika, $1/4$ teaspoon salt, chipotle chili powder and red pepper in blender or food processor. Process just until blended. Transfer to large saucepan. Cook over medium-high heat 5 minutes or until slightly thickened, stirring occasionally. Cool slightly.

4. To serve, drizzle sauce over potatoes or serve sauce in separate bowl for dipping.

NOTE: Sauce can be made up to 24 hours ahead. Cover and refrigerate. Bring to room temperature or reheat before serving.

$2^{1}/_{2}$ pounds small red potatoes, quartered

$1/3$ cup plus 2 tablespoons olive oil, divided

1 teaspoon coarse or kosher salt

$1/2$ teaspoon dried rosemary

1 can (about 14 ounces) diced tomatoes

2 tablespoons red wine vinegar

1 tablespoon minced garlic

1 tablespoon chili powder

1 tablespoon paprika

$1/4$ teaspoon salt

$1/4$ teaspoon chipotle chili powder

$1/8$ to $1/4$ teaspoon ground red pepper

GREEK SALAD

MAKES 4 TO 6 SERVINGS

1. Combine tomatoes, bell pepper, cucumber, onion and olives in large bowl. Top with feta.

2. For dressing, whisk oil, vinegar, garlic, oregano, salt and black pepper in medium bowl until well blended. Pour over salad; stir gently to coat.

GREEK SALAD WITH CHICKEN: To make this classic Mediterranean salad a meal, add seasoned sautéed chicken strips. Combine 1 tablespoon olive oil, 1 teaspoon salt, 1 teaspoon dried oregano, 1 teaspoon paprika, 1/4 teaspoon black pepper and 1 clove garlic, minced, in large bowl. Cut 1 pound chicken tenders in half. Add to spice mixture; toss until well coated. Heat 2 tablespoons olive oil in large skillet over medium-high heat. Add chicken; cook 8 to 10 minutes or until no longer pink, turning once.

SALAD

- 3 medium tomatoes, cut into 8 wedges each and seeds removed
- 1 green bell pepper, cut into 1-inch pieces
- 1/2 English cucumber (8 to 10 inches), quartered lengthwise and sliced crosswise
- 1/2 red onion, thinly sliced
- 1/2 cup pitted kalamata olives
- 1 package (8 ounces) feta cheese, cut into 1/2-inch cubes

DRESSING

- 6 tablespoons extra virgin olive oil
- 3 tablespoons red wine vinegar
- 1 to 2 cloves garlic, minced
- 3/4 teaspoon dried oregano
- 3/4 teaspoon salt
- 1/4 teaspoon black pepper

PARMESAN POTATO WEDGES WITH ROSEMARY AÏOLI

MAKES 6 SERVINGS

1. Preheat oven to 425°F.

2. Cut each potato into 12 wedges. Toss potatoes with oil, salt and pepper in large bowl. Spread in single layer on baking sheet. Bake 20 minutes. Turn and bake an additional 10 minutes or until potatoes are golden brown and tender. Push potatoes together on baking sheet; sprinkle with cheese. Bake additional 5 minutes or until cheese is melted and potatoes are tender.

3. Meanwhile for aïoli, stir together mayonnaise, rosemary, lemon peel and garlic in small bowl. Serve with potatoes.

3 medium baking potatoes

1 tablespoon olive oil

1/2 teaspoon salt

1/8 teaspoon black pepper

1/4 cup shredded Parmesan cheese

1/2 cup mayonnaise

1 teaspoon chopped fresh rosemary *or* 1/2 teaspoon dried rosemary

1/2 teaspoon grated lemon peel

1 clove garlic, minced

MEDITERRANEAN VEGETABLE BAKE

MAKES 4 TO 6 SERVINGS

1. Preheat oven to 350°F. Grease oval casserole or 13×9-inch baking dish.

2. Arrange slices of vegetables in rows, alternating different types and overlapping slices in baking dish to make attractive arrangement; sprinkle evenly with garlic. Combine oil and rosemary in small bowl; drizzle over vegetables.

3. Pour wine over vegetables; season with salt and pepper. Cover loosely with foil. Bake 20 minutes. Uncover; bake 10 to 15 minutes or until vegetables are tender.

2 tomatoes, sliced

1 small red onion, sliced

1 medium zucchini, sliced

1 small eggplant, sliced

1 small yellow squash, sliced

1 large portobello mushroom, sliced

2 cloves garlic, finely chopped

3 tablespoons olive oil

2 teaspoons chopped fresh rosemary leaves

$2/3$ cup dry white wine

Salt and black pepper

ITALIAN-STYLE BROCCOLI

MAKES 4 SERVINGS

1. Trim broccoli, discarding tough stems. Cut broccoli into florets with 2-inch stems. Peel remaining stems; cut into 1/2-inch slices.

2. Bring large saucepan of water to a boil over medium-high heat. Add broccoli; return to a boil. Cook 3 to 5 minutes or until broccoli is tender. Drain; transfer to serving dish.

3. Combine lemon juice, oil, garlic, parsley, salt and pepper in small bowl. Pour over broccoli; toss to coat. Cover and let stand 1 hour before serving to allow flavors to blend. Serve at room temperature.

1¼ **pounds fresh broccoli**

2 **tablespoons lemon juice**

1 **teaspoon extra virgin olive oil**

1 **clove garlic, minced**

1 **teaspoon chopped fresh Italian parsley**

½ **teaspoon salt**

Dash black pepper

FATTOUSH SALAD
MAKES 4 TO 6 SERVINGS

1. Preheat oven to 400°F. Cut pita bread into 1-inch cubes. Toss with 3 tablespoons oil and ½ teaspoon salt in large bowl. Spread on large baking sheet. Bake 10 minutes or until pita cubes are browned and crisp. Cool completely on baking sheet.

2. Combine lettuce, cucumber, tomatoes, green onions, radishes, parsley and mint in large bowl. Add pita cubes.

3. For dressing, whisk remaining ⅓ cup oil, pomegranate molasses, garlic, vinegar and lemon juice in small bowl. Season with remaining ½ teaspoon salt and pepper; whisk until well blended. Taste and adjust seasoning. Pour over salad; toss until well blended.

2 pita breads

⅓ cup plus 3 tablespoons olive oil, divided

1 teaspoon salt, divided

2 cups chopped romaine or green leaf lettuce

1 English cucumber, quartered lengthwise and sliced

2 tomatoes, diced

4 green onions, thinly sliced

3 radishes, thinly sliced

¼ cup finely chopped fresh parsley

1 tablespoon finely chopped fresh mint

2 tablespoons pomegranate molasses or honey

2 cloves garlic, minced

2 tablespoons red wine vinegar

1 tablespoon lemon juice

Black pepper

SHAKSHUKA

MAKES 4 SERVINGS

1. Heat oil in large skillet over medium-high heat. Add bell pepper and onion; cook and stir 3 minutes or until softened. Add garlic, sugar, cumin, paprika, salt and red pepper flakes; cook and stir 1 minute. Stir in tomatoes; mix well. Reduce heat to medium-low. Simmer 15 minutes.

2. Stir in feta. Make 4 divots in tomato mixture. Crack egg into each divot. Cover and cook about 10 minutes or until egg whites are set but yolks are still creamy. Scoop into bowls; sprinkle with cilantro.

2 tablespoons olive oil

1 large red bell pepper, chopped

1 medium onion, chopped

3 cloves garlic, minced

2 teaspoons sugar

2 teaspoons ground cumin

1 teaspoon paprika

½ teaspoon salt

¼ teaspoon crushed red pepper flakes

1 can (28 ounces) crushed tomatoes

¾ cup crumbled feta cheese

4 eggs

Chopped fresh cilantro

HOUSE SALAD
MAKES 4 SERVINGS

1. Prepare croutons, if desired.

2. For dressing, whisk mayonnaise, vinegar, cheese, oil, lemon juice, honey, garlic, Italian seasoning, salt and black pepper in medium bowl until well blended.

3. For salad, place salad blend in large bowl; top with tomatoes, bell pepper, onion, olives and pepperoncini, if desired. Add dressing; toss to coat. Top with croutons.

HOMEMADE CROUTONS: Homemade croutons are incredibly easy to make and much better than store-bought versions. They make a versatile topping for any salad, soup or even pasta dish and keep well in an airtight container at room temperature, so make extras to have on hand. Bonus—croutons are a great way to use up stale bread. If you have stale bread but aren't ready to make croutons, put it in a freezer bag and freeze it until you're ready. Preheat oven to 350°F. Cut any kind of bread into cubes. Hearty bread like whole wheat, Tuscan or sourdough works best, but sandwich bread works, too. Spread the bread on sheet pan and drizzle with olive oil. Toss with spatula or hands to coat. The bread should be evenly coated; add more oil if needed and toss again. If desired, season with salt and pepper and dried herbs like oregano, thyme or rosemary. Bake 10 to 15 minutes or until golden brown, stirring once or twice. Cool on baking sheet before serving.

1 cup homemade croutons (recipe follows) or store-bought croutons

DRESSING

1/2 cup mayonnaise

1/2 cup white wine vinegar

1/4 cup grated Parmesan cheese

1 tablespoon olive oil

1 tablespoon lemon juice

1 tablespoon honey

1 clove garlic, minced

3/4 teaspoon Italian seasoning

1/2 teaspoon salt

1/2 teaspoon black pepper

SALAD

1 package (10 ounces) Italian salad blend

2 plum tomatoes, thinly sliced

1/2 cup thinly sliced red or green bell pepper

1/2 cup thinly sliced red onion

1/4 cup sliced black olives

Pepperoncini (optional)

SOUPS & STEWS

PASTA E FAGIOLI
MAKES 8 SERVINGS

1. Heat oil in Dutch oven over medium heat. Add onion and garlic; cook and stir 5 minutes or until onion is tender.

2. Add tomatoes, broth, beans with liquid, parsley, basil, salt and pepper to Dutch oven; bring to a boil over high heat, stirring occasionally. Reduce heat to low; cover and simmer 10 minutes.

3. Stir in pasta. Cover and simmer 10 minutes or just until pasta is tender. Serve immediately.

2 tablespoons olive oil

1 cup chopped onion

3 cloves garlic, minced

2 cans (about 14 ounces each) Italian-style stewed tomatoes, undrained

3 cups vegetable broth

1 can (about 15 ounces) cannellini beans, undrained

¼ cup chopped fresh Italian parsley

1 teaspoon dried basil

½ teaspoon salt

¼ teaspoon black pepper

4 ounces uncooked small shell pasta

SPICY AFRICAN CHICKPEA AND SWEET POTATO STEW

MAKES 4 SERVINGS

1. Combine garlic and 1 teaspoon salt in food processor; process until garlic is finely chopped. Add paprika, cumin, black pepper, ginger and allspice. Process 15 seconds. With motor running, pour in 1 tablespoon oil through feed tube; process until mixture forms paste.

2. Combine sweet potatoes, broth, chickpeas, tomatoes with juice, okra and spice mixture in large saucepan. Bring to a boil over high heat. Reduce heat to low. Cover and simmer 15 minutes. Uncover; simmer 10 minutes or until vegetables are tender.

3. Meanwhile, heat remaining 1 tablespoon oil in medium saucepan over medium heat. Add green onions; cook and stir 4 minutes. Add water, 1/4 teaspoon salt and saffron. Bring to a boil; stir in couscous. Remove from heat. Cover; let stand 5 minutes. Fluff with fork.

4. Serve stew with couscous and hot pepper sauce.

6 cloves garlic, peeled

1 teaspoon coarse salt

2 teaspoons paprika

1 1/2 teaspoons whole cumin seeds

1 teaspoon black pepper

1/2 teaspoon ground ginger

1/2 teaspoon ground allspice

2 tablespoons olive oil, divided

1 1/2 pounds sweet potatoes, peeled and cubed

2 cups vegetable broth or water

1 can (about 15 ounces) chickpeas, rinsed and drained

1 can (about 14 ounces) plum tomatoes, chopped, juice reserved

1 1/2 cups sliced fresh okra or 1 package (10 ounces) frozen cut okra, thawed

5 green onions, sliced

1 2/3 cups water

1/4 teaspoon salt

1/8 teaspoon saffron threads or 1/2 teaspoon ground turmeric

1 cup uncooked couscous

Hot pepper sauce

MINESTRONE SOUP

MAKES 4 TO 6 SERVINGS

1. Heat oil in large saucepan or Dutch oven over medium-high heat. Add onion, celery, carrot and garlic; cook and stir 5 to 7 minutes or until vegetables are tender. Add broth, bay leaf, salt, basil, oregano, thyme, sugar and pepper; bring to a boil.

2. Stir in kidney beans, navy beans, tomatoes, zucchini, pasta, green beans and wine; cook 10 minutes, stirring occasionally.

3. Add spinach; cook 2 minutes or until pasta and zucchini are tender. Remove and discard bay leaf. Ladle into bowls.

1 tablespoon olive oil

1 medium onion, chopped

1 stalk celery, diced

1 carrot, diced

2 cloves garlic, minced

4 cups vegetable broth

1 bay leaf

1 teaspoon salt

1/2 teaspoon dried basil

1/2 teaspoon dried oregano

1/4 teaspoon dried thyme

1/4 teaspoon sugar

Ground black pepper

1 can (about 15 ounces) dark red kidney beans, rinsed and drained

1 can (about 15 ounces) navy beans or cannellini beans, rinsed and drained

1 can (about 14 ounces) diced tomatoes

1 cup diced zucchini (about 1 small)

1/2 cup uncooked small shell pasta

1/2 cup frozen cut green beans

1/4 cup dry red wine

1 cup packed chopped fresh spinach

ITALIAN WEDDING SOUP

MAKES 8 SERVINGS

1. For meatballs, whisk eggs, 2 cloves garlic, 1 teaspoon salt and black pepper in large bowl until blended. Stir in meat loaf mix, bread crumbs and cheese; mix gently until well blended. Shape mixture by tablespoonfuls into 1-inch balls.

2. Heat oil in large saucepan or Dutch oven over medium heat. Cook meatballs in batches 5 minutes or until browned. Remove to plate; set aside.

3. For soup, add onion, carrots and 4 cloves garlic to saucepan; cook and stir 5 minutes or until onion is lightly browned. Add escarole; cook 2 minutes or until wilted. Stir in broth, tomatoes with juice, thyme, 1 teaspoon salt and red pepper flakes; bring to a boil over high heat. Reduce heat to medium-low; cook 15 minutes.

4. Add meatballs and pasta to soup; return to a boil over high heat. Reduce heat to medium; cook 10 minutes or until pasta is tender. Remove thyme sprigs before serving.

MEATBALLS

- 2 eggs
- 2 cloves garlic, minced
- 1 teaspoon salt
- 1/8 teaspoon black pepper
- 1 1/2 pounds meat loaf mix
- 3/4 cup plain dry bread crumbs
- 1/2 cup grated Parmesan cheese
- 2 tablespoons olive oil

SOUP

- 1 onion, chopped
- 2 carrots, chopped
- 4 cloves garlic, minced
- 2 heads escarole or curly endive, coarsely chopped
- 8 cups chicken broth
- 1 can (about 14 ounces) Italian plum tomatoes, chopped, juice reserved
- 3 fresh thyme sprigs
- 1 teaspoon salt
- 1/2 teaspoon red pepper flakes
- 1 cup uncooked acini di pepe pasta

CIOPPINO

MAKES 4 SERVINGS

1. Heat oil in large saucepan over medium heat. Add onion, celery and garlic; cook and stir 5 minutes or until onion is soft.

2. Add water, Italian seasoning and bouillon; bring to a boil over high heat. Stir in fish and tomato. Reduce heat to medium-low; simmer about 5 minutes or until fish is opaque.

3. Add clams, if desired, shrimp, scallops, crabmeat and lemon juice; simmer about 5 minutes or until shrimp and scallops are opaque. Season with salt and pepper.

1 teaspoon olive oil

1 large onion, chopped

1 cup sliced celery (with celery tops)

1 clove garlic, minced

4 cups water

1 tablespoon Italian seasoning

1 fish-flavored bouillon cube

4 ounces cod or other boneless mild-flavored fish fillets, cut into $\frac{1}{2}$-inch pieces

1 large tomato, chopped

1 can (10 ounces) baby clams, rinsed and drained (optional)

4 ounces small raw shrimp, peeled and deveined

4 ounces raw bay scallops

$\frac{1}{4}$ cup flaked crabmeat or crabmeat blend

2 tablespoons lemon juice

Salt and black pepper

LENTIL SOUP

MAKES 6 TO 8 SERVINGS

1. Heat 1 tablespoon oil in large saucepan or Dutch oven over medium heat. Add onions; cook 10 minutes, stirring occasionally. Add remaining 1 tablespoon oil and salt; cook 10 minutes or until onions are golden brown, stirring frequently.

2. Add garlic; cook and stir 1 minute. Add tomato paste, oregano, basil, thyme and pepper; cook and stir 1 minute. Stir in sherry; cook 30 seconds, scraping up browned bits from bottom of saucepan.

3. Stir in broth, water, carrots and lentils; cover and bring to a boil over high heat. Reduce heat to medium-low; cook, partially covered, 30 minutes or until lentils are tender.

4. Remove from heat; stir in parsley and vinegar.

2 tablespoons olive oil, divided

2 medium onions, chopped

$1\frac{1}{2}$ teaspoons salt

4 cloves garlic, minced

$\frac{1}{4}$ cup tomato paste

1 teaspoon dried oregano

$\frac{1}{2}$ teaspoon dried basil

$\frac{1}{4}$ teaspoon dried thyme

$\frac{1}{4}$ teaspoon black pepper

$\frac{1}{2}$ cup dry sherry or white wine

8 cups vegetable broth

2 cups water

3 carrots, cut into $\frac{1}{2}$-inch pieces

2 cups dried lentils, rinsed and sorted

1 cup chopped fresh parsley

1 tablespoon balsamic vinegar

PASTA

PASTA PUTTANESCA

MAKES 4 SERVINGS

1. Heat oil in large skillet over medium heat. Add onion; cook and stir about 2 minutes or until translucent. Add capers, garlic, Italian seasoning, bay leaf and red pepper flakes, if desired; cook and stir about 1 minute or until aromatic.

2. Add tomatoes with juice, tuna and olives, stirring to break up tuna into chunks. Cook about 5 minutes or until heated through. Just before serving, stir in parsley and lemon juice. Remove and discard bay leaf. Taste and season with salt.

3. Divide spaghetti among serving bowls; top evenly with sauce. Sprinkle each serving with 1 tablespoon cheese.

- 1 tablespoon olive oil
- 1/2 cup chopped onion
- 2 teaspoons capers, drained
- 1 clove garlic, minced
- 1 teaspoon Italian seasoning
- 1 bay leaf

  Pinch red pepper flakes or few drops hot pepper sauce (optional)

- 1 can (about 14 ounces) diced tomatoes, undrained
- 1 can (about 6 ounces) water-packed solid white albacore tuna, drained
- 1/4 cup pitted kalamata olives
- 3 tablespoons chopped fresh Italian parsley

  Juice of 1/2 lemon

  Salt

- 2 cups hot cooked multigrain spaghetti
- 1/4 cup shredded Parmesan cheese

SPICED CHICKPEAS AND COUSCOUS

MAKES 6 SERVINGS

1. Combine broth, coriander, cardamom, turmeric, hot pepper sauce, salt and cinnamon in large saucepan; bring to a boil over high heat. Add carrots; reduce heat and simmer 5 minutes.

2. Add chickpeas and green peas; return to a simmer. Simmer, uncovered, 2 minutes.

3. Stir in couscous. Cover; remove from heat. Let stand 5 minutes or until liquid is absorbed. Sprinkle with mint.

1 can (about 14 ounces) vegetable broth

1 teaspoon ground coriander

1/2 teaspoon ground cardamom

1/2 teaspoon ground turmeric

1/2 teaspoon hot pepper sauce

1/4 teaspoon salt

1/8 teaspoon ground cinnamon

1 cup matchstick-size carrots

1 can (15 ounces) chickpeas, rinsed and drained

1 cup frozen green peas

1 cup uncooked couscous

2 tablespoons chopped fresh mint or parsley

VEGETABLE PENNE ITALIANO

MAKES 4 SERVINGS

1. Heat oil in large skillet over medium-high heat. Add bell peppers, onion and garlic; cook and stir 8 minutes or until vegetables are crisp-tender.

2. Add tomato paste, salt, sugar, Italian seasoning and black pepper; cook and stir 1 minute. Stir in tomatoes with juice. Reduce heat to medium-low; cook 15 minutes or until vegetables are tender and sauce is thickened.

3. Meanwhile, cook pasta in large saucepan of salted water according to package directions for al dente. Drain pasta; return to saucepan. Add sauce; stir gently to coat. Divide among serving bowls; top with cheese and basil.

1 tablespoon olive oil

1 red bell pepper, cut into 1/2-inch pieces

1 green bell pepper, cut into 1/2-inch pieces

1 medium sweet onion, halved and thinly sliced

3 cloves garlic, minced

2 tablespoons tomato paste

2 teaspoons salt

1 teaspoon sugar

1 teaspoon Italian seasoning

1/4 teaspoon black pepper

1 can (28 ounces) Italian plum tomatoes, chopped, juice reserved

8 ounces uncooked penne pasta

Grated Parmesan cheese

Chopped fresh basil

PASTA E CECI

MAKES 4 SERVINGS

1. Heat 3 tablespoons oil in large saucepan over medium-high heat. Add onion and carrot; cook and stir 10 minutes or until vegetables are softened.

2. Add garlic, rosemary and 1½ teaspoons salt; cook and stir 1 minute. Add chickpeas with liquid, broth, tomatoes, bay leaf and red pepper flakes. Remove 1 cup mixture; place in food processor or blender. Process until smooth. Stir back into saucepan; bring to a boil.

3. Add pasta; reduce heat to medium and cook 12 to 15 minutes or until pasta is tender and mixture is creamy. Remove bay leaf and rosemary sprig. Taste and season with additional salt and black pepper, if desired. Divide among bowls; garnish with parsley and drizzle with remaining 1 tablespoon oil.

TIP: To easily crush whole canned tomatoes into the perfect consistency, squeeze them through your fingers over the saucepan.

4 tablespoons olive oil, divided

1 onion, chopped

1 carrot, chopped

1 clove garlic, minced

1 fresh rosemary sprig

1½ teaspoons salt

1 can (15 ounces) chickpeas, undrained

2 cups vegetable broth or water

1 can (28 ounces) whole tomatoes, drained and crushed

1 bay leaf

⅛ teaspoon red pepper flakes

1 cup uncooked orecchiette

Black pepper

Chopped fresh parsley or basil

PASTA AND POTATOES WITH PESTO

MAKES 4 TO 6 SERVINGS

1. For pesto, place basil, pine nuts, garlic, salt and pepper in food processor. With motor running, add oil in thin steady stream; process until evenly blended and pine nuts are finely chopped. Add 1/4 cup cheese; pulse just until blended.

2. Place potatoes in medium saucepan of salted water. Bring to a boil over high heat; reduce heat. Cook, uncovered, 10 minutes or until potatoes are tender; drain.

3. Meanwhile, cook linguine in large saucepan of salted water according to package directions, adding peas during last 3 minutes of cooking. Drain and return pasta mixture to pan. Add potatoes, pesto and remaining 1/4 cup cheese; toss until well blended. Season with salt and pepper, if desired.

1 cup tightly packed fresh basil leaves

1/4 cup pine nuts

2 cloves garlic

1/2 teaspoon salt

1/4 teaspoon black pepper

1/4 cup extra virgin olive oil

1/2 cup shredded Parmesan cheese, divided

3 medium red potatoes, cut into chunks

8 ounces uncooked linguine

3/4 cup frozen peas or fresh green beans (1-inch pieces)

Salt and black pepper (optional)

GREEN BEAN, WALNUT AND BLUE CHEESE PASTA

MAKES 6 SERVINGS

1. Cook pasta according to package directions in large saucepan of boiling salted water until al dente. Add green beans during last 4 minutes of cooking. Drain. Place in large bowl.

2. Meanwhile, whisk oil, vinegar, thyme, mustard, lemon juice, honey, salt and pepper in medium bowl until smooth and well blended.

3. Pour dressing over pasta and green beans; toss to coat evenly. Stir in walnuts and cheese. Serve warm or cover and refrigerate until ready to serve.**

**If serving cold, stir walnuts into salad just before serving.

- 2 cups uncooked gemelli pasta
- 2 cups trimmed halved green beans
- 3 tablespoons extra virgin olive oil
- 2 tablespoons white wine vinegar
- 1 tablespoon chopped fresh thyme *or* 1 teaspoon dried thyme
- 1 tablespoon Dijon mustard
- 1 tablespoon fresh lemon juice
- 1 teaspoon honey
- ¼ teaspoon salt
- ¼ teaspoon black pepper
- ½ cup chopped walnuts, toasted*
- ½ cup crumbled blue cheese

*To toast walnuts, spread in single layer in heavy skillet. Cook over medium heat 2 to 3 minutes or until lightly browned, stirring frequently.

LENTIL BOLOGNESE

MAKES 6 TO 8 SERVINGS

1. Heat oil in large saucepan over medium heat. Add onion, carrot and celery; cook and stir 10 minutes or until onion is lightly browned and carrots are softened.

2. Stir in salt, oregano and red pepper flakes. Add tomato paste; cook and stir 1 minute. Add wine; cook and stir until absorbed. Stir in crushed tomatoes, diced tomatoes, lentils, mushroom and water. Bring to a simmer.

3. Reduce heat to medium; partially cover and simmer about 40 minutes or until lentils are tender, removing cover after 20 minutes. Serve over pasta.

2 tablespoons olive oil

1 onion, chopped

1 carrot, chopped

1 stalk celery, chopped

1 teaspoon salt

1/2 teaspoon dried oregano

   Pinch red pepper flakes

3 tablespoons tomato paste

1/4 cup dry white wine

1 can (28 ounces) crushed tomatoes

1 can (about 14 ounces) diced tomatoes

1 cup dried lentils, rinsed and sorted

1 portobello mushroom, gills removed, finely chopped

1 1/2 cups water or vegetable broth

8 ounces whole wheat pasta, cooked according to package directions

SPAGHETTI WITH CAULIFLOWER AND FETA

MAKES 4 SERVINGS

1. Heat oil in large skillet over medium heat. Add onion; cook and stir 3 minutes or until soft. Add garlic; cook and stir 2 minutes. Add cauliflower; cook and stir 5 minutes. Add wine, salt and pepper. Cover and cook about 15 minutes or until cauliflower is crisp-tender.

2. Meanwhile, cook pasta according to package directions in large saucepan of boiling salted water until al dente. Reserve $1/2$ cup pasta cooking water; drain pasta and keep warm.

3. Add tomatoes, walnuts and reserved pasta water to skillet; season with red pepper flakes, if desired. Cook 2 to 3 minutes or until tomatoes begin to soften.

4. Toss spaghetti with cauliflower mixture in skillet or serving bowl; top with feta.

3 tablespoons olive oil

1 onion, chopped

4 cloves garlic, minced

1 head cauliflower, cut into bite-size florets

$2/3$ cup dry white wine

1 teaspoon salt

$1/2$ teaspoon black pepper

6 ounces uncooked whole wheat spaghetti

1 pint grape tomatoes, halved

$1/2$ cup coarsely chopped walnuts

$1/4$ teaspoon red pepper flakes (optional)

$1/2$ cup crumbled feta cheese

PASTA WITH ONIONS AND GOAT CHEESE

MAKES 4 SERVINGS

1. Heat oil in large nonstick skillet over medium heat. Add onions and $1/2$ teaspoon salt; cook about 20 to 25 minutes or until golden and caramelized, stirring occasionally.

2. Combine goat cheese and milk in small bowl; mash and stir until well blended. Set aside.

3. Cook pasta according to package directions in large saucepan of boiling salted water until al dente. Drain and set aside.

4. Add garlic to onions in skillet; cook about 3 minutes or until softened. Add wine, sage, remaining $1/2$ teaspoon salt and pepper; cook until liquid has evaporated. Remove from heat. Add pasta and goat cheese mixture; stir until cheese is melted. Sprinkle with walnuts.

1 tablespoon olive oil

3 to 4 cups thinly sliced sweet onions (2 large onions)

1 teaspoon salt, divided

$3/4$ cup (3 ounces) crumbled goat cheese

$1/4$ cup milk

8 ounces uncooked campanelle or farfalle pasta

1 clove garlic, minced

2 tablespoons dry white wine or vegetable broth

$1^{1}/2$ teaspoons chopped fresh sage *or* $1/2$ teaspoon dried sage

$1/4$ teaspoon black pepper

$1/2$ cup chopped toasted walnuts

ROASTED SQUASH WITH TAHINI COUSCOUS

MAKES 4 TO 6 SERVINGS

1. Preheat oven to 400°F. Toss squash, 1 tablespoon oil and 1 teaspoon salt in medium bowl; spread on sheet pan. Bake 30 minutes or until squash is tender and browned, stirring once or twice.

2. Heat remaining 1 tablespoon oil in medium skillet over high heat. Add couscous; cook and stir 2 to 3 minutes or until some of couscous is lightly browned. Stir in 1/2 teaspoon salt. Add 2 1/2 cups water; bring to a boil. Reduce heat to medium; cook about 10 minutes or until water is mostly absorbed, stirring occasionally. Remove from heat. Cover and let stand 5 minutes or until water is absorbed and couscous is tender.

3. Whisk tahini, maple syrup, paprika and remaining 1/4 teaspoon salt in small bowl. Whisk in remaining 1/4 cup water until smooth. Stir into couscous. Add squash and preserved lemon; stir gently. Sprinkle with almonds; garnish with parsley. Serve warm.

1 butternut squash (about 2 1/2 pounds), peeled and cut into 1/2-inch cubes

2 tablespoons olive oil, divided

1 3/4 teaspoons salt, divided

1 package (6 ounces) plain pearled couscous (1 cup)

2 3/4 cups water, divided

1/2 cup tahini

1 tablespoon maple syrup

1/4 teaspoon smoked paprika

1/4 cup chopped preserved lemon

1/4 cup chopped almonds

Minced fresh parsley (optional)

RICE, BEANS & GRAINS

RISI BISI

MAKES 6 SERVINGS

1. Heat oil in large saucepan over medium-high heat. Add onion; cook and stir 5 minutes or until soft but not browned. Add garlic, salt, basil and oregano; cook and stir 30 seconds.

2. Add rice; cook and stir 2 to 3 minutes or until rice is toasted. Add broth; bring to a boil. Reduce heat to medium; simmer 15 minutes or until rice is tender and broth is absorbed. Stir in peas; cook 2 to 3 minutes or until peas are heated through. Stir in cheese. Sprinkle with pine nuts, if desired.

- 2 tablespoons olive oil
- 1 cup chopped onion
- 2 cloves garlic, minced
- 1 teaspoon salt
- $\frac{1}{2}$ teaspoon dried basil
- $\frac{1}{2}$ teaspoon dried oregano
- 1$\frac{1}{2}$ cups uncooked medium or long grain rice, rinsed well in fine-mesh strainer
- 3 cups vegetable broth
- $\frac{1}{2}$ cup frozen peas
- $\frac{1}{2}$ cup grated Parmesan cheese
- $\frac{1}{4}$ cup toasted pine nuts (optional)

ROASTED CHICKPEA AND SWEET POTATO BOWL

MAKES 2 SERVINGS

1. Preheat oven to 350°F.

2. Peel sweet potato and cut in half. Using spiralizer, cut sweet potato into ribbons with thin ribbon blade. Cut into 3-inch pieces. Place in 13×9-inch pan. Drizzle with 1 teaspoon oil and sprinkle with ¼ teaspoon salt and pepper; toss to coat. Push to one side of pan.

3. Combine chickpeas, maple syrup, remaining 1 tablespoon oil, paprika, cumin and ½ teaspoon salt in medium bowl; toss to coat. Spread in other side of pan. Bake 30 minutes, stirring potatoes and chickpeas once or twice.

4. Meanwhile, bring quinoa, 1 cup water and remaining ¼ teaspoon salt to a boil in small saucepan. Reduce heat to low; cover and simmer 15 minutes or until quinoa is tender and water is absorbed.

5. For sauce, whisk tahini, lemon juice, 2 tablespoons water, garlic and ⅛ teaspoon salt in small bowl until smooth. Add additional water if needed to reach desired consistency.

6. Divide quinoa between two bowls. Top with sweet potatoes, chickpeas and sauce. Sprinkle with parsley.

NOTE: If you don't have a spiralizer, julienne the sweet potato or cut it into cubes instead.

1 sweet potato

1 tablespoon plus 1 teaspoon olive oil, divided

1 teaspoon salt, divided

Black pepper

1 can (about 15 ounces) chickpeas, rinsed, drained and patted dry

1 tablespoon maple syrup

1 teaspoon paprika, sweet or smoked

½ teaspoon ground cumin

½ cup uncooked quinoa, rinsed well in fine-mesh strainer

1 cup water

Minced fresh parsley or cilantro

TAHINI SAUCE

¼ cup tahini

2 tablespoons lemon juice

2 tablespoons water

1 clove garlic, minced

⅛ teaspoon salt

CHEESY POLENTA

MAKES 6 SERVINGS

1. Coat inside of slow cooker with nonstick cooking spray. Heat broth in large saucepan over high heat. Remove to slow cooker; whisk in polenta.

2. Cover; cook on LOW 2 to 2½ hours or until polenta is tender and creamy. Stir in ½ cup cheese and butter. Serve with additional cheese. Garnish with sage.

TIP: To make polenta on the stove, bring broth to a boil in large saucepan over high heat. Gradually whisk in polenta in thin steady stream. Cook 2 to 3 minutes or until thickened, whisking frequently. Reduce heat to low; cook about 45 minutes, stirring occasionally and adding water ½ cup at a time if polenta seems dry. Stir in cheese and butter just before serving. Spread any leftover polenta in a baking dish and refrigerate until cold. Cut cold polenta into sticks or slices. You can then fry or grill the polenta until lightly browned.

6 cups vegetable broth

1½ cups uncooked medium-grind instant polenta

½ cup grated Parmesan cheese, plus additional for serving

¼ cup (½ stick) unsalted butter, cubed

Fried sage leaves (optional)

FARRO, GRAPE AND ROASTED CARROT BOWL

MAKES 4 TO 6 SERVINGS

1. Preheat oven to 375°F. Place carrots on sheet pan. Drizzle with 1 tablespoon oil. Combine 1/2 teaspoon salt, cumin, coriander and nutmeg in small bowl; sprinkle over carrots. Toss to coat carrots with oil and spices. Arrange cut sides down in single layer.

2. Roast 30 minutes or until carrots are browned and tender, turning once. Place almonds on small baking sheet; bake about 5 minutes or until almonds are toasted, stirring frequently.

3. Meanwhile, bring 2 cups water and remaining 1/2 teaspoon salt to a boil in medium saucepan. Stir in farro; reduce heat to medium-low. Cover and simmer 25 minutes or until tender. Drain and place farro in large bowl.

4. Whisk remaining 3 tablespoons oil into vinegar in small bowl; pour over farro. Stir in grapes and onion; season to taste with additional salt and pepper. Cut carrots into 1-inch pieces; add to farro mixture. Place greens in bowls; top with farro salad and sprinkle with almonds.

1 pound carrots, peeled, trimmed and halved lengthwise

4 tablespoons extra virgin olive oil, divided

1 teaspoon salt, divided

1/2 teaspoon ground cumin

1/4 teaspoon ground coriander

1/8 teaspoon ground nutmeg

1 package (2 1/4 ounces) slivered almonds

2 cups water

1 cup uncooked pearled farro, rinsed under cold water

2 tablespoons balsamic vinegar

1 cup halved red grapes

1/4 cup minced red onion

4 cups mixed spring greens

Salt and black pepper

PARMESAN POLENTA

MAKES 6 SERVINGS

1. Spray 11×7-inch baking pan with nonstick cooking spray. Spray one side of 7-inch-long sheet of waxed paper with cooking spray.

2. Combine broth, onion, garlic, rosemary and salt in medium saucepan; bring to a boil over high heat. Add cornmeal gradually, stirring constantly. Reduce heat to medium; simmer 30 minutes or until mixture has consistency of thick mashed potatoes. Remove from heat; stir in cheese.

3. Spread polenta evenly in prepared pan; place waxed paper, sprayed side down, on polenta and smooth surface. (If surface is bumpy, it is more likely to stick to grill.) Cool on wire rack 15 minutes or until firm. Remove waxed paper; cut into 6 squares and remove from pan.

4. Spray grid with cooking spray. Preheat grill. Brush tops of polenta squares with half of oil. Grill polenta, oil side down on covered grill over low to medium heat 6 to 8 minutes or until golden. Brush with remaining oil; turn and grill 6 to 8 minutes or until golden. Serve warm.

4 cups vegetable broth

1 small onion, minced

4 cloves garlic, minced

1 tablespoon minced fresh rosemary *or* 1 teaspoon dried rosemary

1/2 teaspoon salt

1 1/4 cups yellow cornmeal

6 tablespoons grated Parmesan cheese

1 tablespoon olive oil, divided

BUCKWHEAT WITH ZUCCHINI AND MUSHROOMS

MAKES 6 SERVINGS

1. Heat oil in large nonstick skillet over medium heat. Add mushrooms, zucchini, onion and garlic; cook and stir 7 to 10 minutes or until vegetables are tender. Add buckwheat, thyme, salt and pepper; cook and stir 2 minutes.

2. Add broth; bring to a boil. Cover; reduce heat to low. Cook 10 to 13 minutes or until liquid is absorbed and buckwheat is tender. Remove from heat; let stand, covered, 5 minutes. Serve with lemon wedges, if desired.

2 tablespoons olive oil

1 cup sliced mushrooms

1 medium zucchini, cut into 1/2-inch pieces

1 medium onion, chopped

1 clove garlic, minced

3/4 cup buckwheat

1/4 teaspoon dried thyme

1/4 teaspoon salt

1/8 teaspoon black pepper

1 1/4 cups vegetable broth

Lemon wedges (optional)

LENTILS WITH WALNUTS

MAKES 4 TO 6 SERVINGS

1. Place walnuts in medium saucepan. Cook and stir over medium heat 2 to 3 minutes or until fragrant and toasted. Transfer to plate.

2. Heat oil in same saucepan over medium-high heat. Add carrot, celery and shallot; cook and stir 3 minutes or until vegetables are softened. Stir in salt and thyme; cook 10 seconds. Add broth, lentils and bay leaf; bring to a boil.

3. Reduce heat to medium; simmer 15 to 20 minutes or until lentils are tender and most of broth is absorbed. Remove bay leaf. Stir in vinegar. Top with walnuts.

$\frac{1}{4}$ cup chopped walnuts

1 tablespoon olive oil

1 carrot, chopped

1 stalk celery, chopped

1 shallot, chopped

$\frac{1}{2}$ teaspoon salt

$\frac{1}{4}$ teaspoon dried thyme

3 cups vegetable broth

1 cup dried brown lentils, rinsed and sorted

1 bay leaf

2 teaspoons red wine vinegar

TABBOULEH

MAKES 8 SERVINGS

1. Rinse bulgur thoroughly in colander under cold water, picking out any debris; drain well. Transfer to medium heatproof bowl. Stir in boiling water and salt. Cover; let stand 30 minutes. Drain well.

2. Combine lemon juice, oil, basil and black pepper in small bowl. Pour over bulgur; mix well.

3. Layer bulgur, green onion, cucumber, bell pepper and tomato in medium bowl; sprinkle with parsley and mint.

4. Cover and refrigerate at least 2 hours to allow flavors to blend. Toss before serving.

½ **cup uncooked bulgur wheat**

¾ **cup boiling water**

½ **teaspoon salt**

5 **teaspoons lemon juice**

2 **teaspoons extra virgin olive oil**

½ **teaspoon dried basil**

¼ **teaspoon black pepper**

1 **green onion, thinly sliced**

½ **cup chopped cucumber**

½ **cup chopped green bell pepper**

½ **cup chopped tomato**

¼ **cup chopped fresh parsley**

2 **teaspoons chopped fresh mint**

MUJADARA
MAKES 4 TO 6 SERVINGS

1. Place lentils in medium saucepan; cover with water by 1 inch. Bring to a boil over medium-high heat. Reduce heat to medium-low; simmer 10 minutes. Drain and rinse under cold water.

2. Meanwhile, heat ¼ cup oil in large saucepan or Dutch oven. Add onions and 1 teaspoon salt; cook and stir 15 minutes or until golden and parts are crispy. Remove most of onions to small bowl, leaving about ½ cup in saucepan.*

3. Add remaining 1 tablespoon oil to saucepan with onions; heat over medium-high heat. Add cumin, allspice, cinnamon stick, bay leaf and red pepper; cook and stir 30 seconds. Add rice; cook and stir 2 to 3 minutes or until rice is lightly toasted. Add broth, lentils and 1 teaspoon salt; bring to a boil. Reduce heat to low; cover and cook about 15 minutes or until broth is absorbed and rice and lentils are tender. Remove saucepan from heat. Place clean kitchen towel over top of saucepan; replace lid and let stand 5 to 10 minutes.

4. Meanwhile, peel cucumber and trim ends. Grate cucumber on large holes of box grater; squeeze out excess liquid. Place in medium bowl; stir in yogurt and remaining ½ teaspoon salt. Serve lentils and rice with reserved onions and cucumber sauce.

If desired, continue to cook reserved onions in a medium skillet over medium heat until dark golden brown.

1 **cup dried brown lentils, rinsed and sorted**

¼ **cup plus 1 tablespoon olive oil, divided**

2 **sweet onions, thinly sliced**

2½ **teaspoons salt, divided**

1½ **teaspoons ground cumin**

1 **teaspoon ground allspice**

1 **cinnamon stick**

1 **bay leaf**

¼ **teaspoon ground red pepper**

¾ **cup long grain white rice, rinsed well in fine-mesh strainer**

3 **cups vegetable broth or water**

1 **cucumber**

1 **cup plain Greek yogurt or sour cream**

SPINACH AND MUSHROOM RISOTTO

MAKES 8 SERVINGS

1. Heat oil in large saucepan over medium-high heat. Add mushrooms, basil, garlic and pepper; cook and stir 5 minutes or until mushrooms are tender.

2. Add rice and salt; cook and stir 2 to 3 minutes or until rice is translucent. Add wine; cook and stir until absorbed. Add broth, ¹/₂ cup at a time, stirring until broth is absorbed before adding next addition. Add spinach with last ¹/₂ cup broth; cook and stir until broth is absorbed.

3. Cover and let stand 5 to 7 minutes or until spinach is wilted. Sprinkle with walnuts and cheese before serving.

¹/₄ cup olive oil

8 ounces mushrooms, sliced

2 teaspoons dried basil

2 teaspoons minced garlic

¹/₄ teaspoon black pepper

1¹/₂ cups uncooked arborio rice

1 teaspoon salt

¹/₂ cup dry white wine

4 cups vegetable broth

3 cups packed stemmed spinach, chopped

6 tablespoons chopped walnuts, toasted*

¹/₄ cup grated Parmesan cheese

To toast walnuts, spread in single layer in heavy skillet. Cook over medium heat 2 to 3 minutes or until lightly browned, stirring frequently.

CHICKEN & MEAT

ROAST CHICKEN AND POTATOES CATALAN

MAKES 4 SERVINGS

1. Preheat oven to 400°F. Spray large shallow roasting pan or sheet pan with nonstick cooking spray.

2. Combine oil, lemon juice, thyme, salt, ground red pepper and saffron in large bowl; mix well. Add potatoes; toss to coat.

3. Arrange potatoes in single layer around edges of pan. Place chicken in center of pan; brush both sides of chicken with remaining oil mixture in bowl.

4. Bake 20 minutes. Turn potatoes; baste chicken with pan juices. Add bell pepper; continue baking 20 minutes or until chicken is no longer pink in center, juices run clear and potatoes are browned. Stir peas into potato mixture; bake 5 minutes or until heated through. Garnish with lemon wedges.

2 tablespoons olive oil

2 tablespoons lemon juice

1 teaspoon dried thyme

$\frac{1}{2}$ teaspoon salt

$\frac{1}{4}$ teaspoon ground red pepper

$\frac{1}{4}$ teaspoon ground saffron or $\frac{1}{2}$ teaspoon crushed saffron threads or turmeric

2 large baking potatoes (about 1$\frac{1}{2}$ pounds), cut into 1$\frac{1}{2}$-inch pieces

4 skinless bone-in chicken breasts (about 2 pounds)

1 cup sliced red bell pepper

1 cup frozen peas, thawed

Lemon wedges

SPICED CHICKEN SKEWERS WITH YOGURT-TAHINI SAUCE

MAKES 8 SERVINGS

1. Spray grid with nonstick cooking spray. Prepare grill for direct cooking.

2. For sauce, combine yogurt, 1/4 cup parsley, tahini, lemon juice, garlic and 1/4 teaspoon salt in food processor or blender; process until smooth. Set aside.

3. Combine oil, garam masala and remaining 1/2 teaspoon salt in medium bowl. Add chicken; toss to coat. Thread chicken on 8 (6-inch) wooden or metal skewers.

4. Grill chicken skewers over medium-high heat 5 minutes per side or until chicken is no longer pink. Serve with sauce. Garnish with additional parsley.

1 cup plain Greek yogurt

1/4 cup chopped fresh parsley, plus additional for garnish

1/4 cup tahini

2 tablespoons lemon juice

1 clove garlic

3/4 teaspoon salt, divided

1 tablespoon olive oil

2 teaspoons garam masala

1 pound boneless skinless chicken breasts, cut into 1-inch pieces

TUSCAN LAMB SKILLET

MAKES 4 SERVINGS

1. Trim fat from lamb chops. Heat oil in large skillet over medium heat. Add lamb; cook about 4 minutes per side or until 160°F for medium doneness. Transfer to plate; keep warm.

2. Stir garlic into drippings in skillet; cook and stir 1 minute. Stir in beans, tomatoes with liquid, vinegar and minced rosemary; bring to a boil. Reduce heat to medium-low; simmer 5 minutes.

3. Divide bean mixture among serving plates; top with lamb.

8 lamb rib chops (1½ pounds), cut 1 inch thick

2 teaspoons olive oil

3 teaspoons minced garlic

1 can (29 ounces) cannellini beans, rinsed and drained

1 can (about 14 ounces) Italian-style tomatoes, broken up, juice reserved

1 tablespoon balsamic vinegar

2 teaspoons minced fresh rosemary

GREEK CHICKEN

MAKES 4 SERVINGS

1. Preheat oven to 375°F. Arrange garlic in shallow roasting pan. Place chicken over garlic. Combine 2 tablespoons lemon juice, oil and rosemary in small bowl; spoon evenly over chicken. Sprinkle chicken with salt and pepper.

2. Bake 50 to 55 minutes or until chicken is cooked through (165°F). Remove to serving platter; tent with foil to keep warm.

3. Squeeze garlic pulp from skins into roasting pan; add remaining 2 tablespoons lemon juice. Cook over medium heat, mashing garlic and scraping up browned bits from bottom of pan. Pour sauce over chicken; sprinkle with lemon peel. Garnish with rosemary sprigs and lemon.

TIP: Unpeeled cloves of garlic usually burst open while roasting, making it a cinch to squeeze out the softened, creamy roasted garlic with your thumb and forefinger. If the cloves have not burst open, simply slice off the end with a knife and squeeze out the garlic.

12 cloves garlic, unpeeled

3 pounds chicken thighs and drumsticks

4 tablespoons lemon juice, divided

3 tablespoons olive oil

2 tablespoons chopped fresh rosemary leaves *or* 2 teaspoons dried rosemary

3/4 teaspoon salt

1/2 teaspoon black pepper

1 teaspoon grated lemon peel

Additional sprigs fresh rosemary and lemon wedges

MOROCCAN CHICKEN MEATBALLS WITH APRICOTS AND ALMONDS

MAKES 4 TO 6 SERVINGS

1. Preheat oven to 325°F.

2. Combine chicken, 1/2 teaspoon salt, cinnamon and black pepper in medium bowl. Shape into 1-inch balls. Heat oil in large skillet. Add meatballs; brown on all sides. Remove to plate.

3. Add onion and apricots to skillet; cook and stir 5 minutes over medium heat or until onion is tender. Stir in tomatoes, remaining 1/4 teaspoon salt, red pepper flakes and ginger. Simmer 5 minutes.

4. Meanwhile, bring broth to a boil in small saucepan. Stir in couscous. Reduce heat; cover and simmer 10 minutes or until couscous is tender and almost all liquid has been absorbed. Drain if necessary.

5. Grease 11×7-inch baking dish. Place couscous in dish; top with meatballs and tomato mixture. Bake 20 minutes or until chicken is cooked through. Sprinkle with almonds.

1 pound ground chicken*

3/4 teaspoon salt, divided

1/4 teaspoon ground cinnamon

1/4 teaspoon black pepper

1 tablespoon olive oil

1 small onion, chopped

1 cup sliced dried apricots

1 can (28 ounces) diced tomatoes

1/2 teaspoon red pepper flakes

1/2 teaspoon ground ginger

1 1/2 cups chicken broth

1 cup plain pearled couscous

1/4 cup sliced almonds, toasted**

*Or substitute ground turkey or lamb.

**To toast almonds, spread in single layer in heavy skillet. Cook over medium heat 2 to 3 minutes or until lightly browned, stirring frequently.

TUSCAN PORK LOIN ROAST WITH FIG SAUCE

MAKES 6 TO 8 SERVINGS

1. Preheat oven to 350°F. Combine oil, garlic, salt, rosemary and red pepper flakes in small bowl; brush over roast. Place pork on rack in shallow roasting pan.

2. Roast 45 minutes or until internal temperature is 145°F. Transfer to cutting board. Tent with foil; let stand 10 minutes.

3. Meanwhile, pour wine into roasting pan; cook over medium-high heat 2 minutes, stirring to scrape up browned bits. Stir in fig jam; cook and stir until heated through. Cut pork into thin slices; serve with sauce.

2 tablespoons olive oil

3 cloves garlic, minced

2 teaspoons coarse salt

2 teaspoons dried rosemary

$1/2$ teaspoon red pepper flakes *or* 1 teaspoon black pepper

1 center cut boneless pork loin roast (about 3 pounds)

$1/4$ cup dry red wine

1 jar (about 8 ounces) fig jam

PERSIAN ROAST CHICKEN WITH WALNUT-POMEGRANATE SAUCE

MAKES 4 SERVINGS

1. Preheat oven to 375°F. Spray shallow roasting pan with nonstick cooking spray.

2. Combine 1 tablespoon cumin, lemon juice, lemon peel, 1 teaspoon salt, turmeric, 1/4 teaspoon saffron, 1/4 teaspoon pepper and cinnamon in small bowl; mix well to form paste. Rub mixture over chicken to lightly coat.

3. Heat 2 tablespoons oil in large skillet over medium-high heat. Add chicken in single layer (cook in batches if necessary); cook until lightly browned, about 4 minutes per side. Transfer to prepared pan. Roast 25 to 28 minutes or until thermometer inserted into thickest part of each piece registers 165°F.

4. Meanwhile, heat remaining 1 tablespoon oil in medium skillet over medium-high heat. Add onions; cook and stir 10 to 15 minutes or until golden brown. Add pomegranate juice, sugar, remaining 1/2 teaspoon cumin and remaining 1/8 teaspoon saffron; bring to a boil.

5. Cook 10 to 11 minutes or until mixture is syrupy and reduced by about half, stirring occasionally. Remove from heat. Stir in walnuts; season with remaining 1/4 teaspoon salt and 1/4 teaspoon pepper. Serve over chicken; garnish with pomegranate seeds.

1 tablespoon plus 1/2 teaspoon ground cumin, divided

1 tablespoon fresh lemon juice

2 teaspoons grated lemon peel

1 1/4 teaspoons salt, divided

1 teaspoon ground turmeric

1/4 teaspoon plus 1/8 teaspoon saffron threads, lightly crushed, divided

1/2 teaspoon black pepper, divided

1/8 teaspoon ground cinnamon

1 chicken, cut up (about 5 pounds)

3 tablespoons olive oil, divided

2 cups thinly sliced onions

2 cups unsweetened pomegranate juice

1/2 cup sugar

1/4 cup walnuts, finely chopped

Pomegranate seeds (optional)

ITALIAN COUNTRY-STYLE BRAISED CHICKEN

MAKES 4 TO 6 SERVINGS

1. Combine boiling water and mushrooms in small bowl. Let stand 15 to 20 minutes or until mushrooms are tender.

2. Meanwhile, combine flour, salt and pepper in large resealable food storage bag. Add 1 or 2 pieces of chicken at a time; toss to coat. Discard any remaining flour mixture.

3. Heat oil in large skillet over medium heat. Brown chicken on both sides. Transfer chicken to plate; set aside.

4. Pour off all but 1 tablespoon oil from skillet. Add pancetta, onion and carrots; cook 5 minutes, stirring occasionally to scrape up browned bits. Add garlic; cook and stir 1 minute.

5. Drain mushrooms, reserving liquid. Chop mushrooms. Add mushrooms and reserved liquid to skillet. Add broth and tomato paste; bring to a boil over high heat.

6. Return chicken to skillet with any juices from plate. Reduce heat to low; simmer 20 minutes or until chicken is cooked through (165°F) and sauce thickens, turning once. Stir in olives; cook and stir until heated through. Transfer chicken to serving platter; top with sauce.

³/₄ cup boiling water

¹/₂ cup dried porcini mushrooms (about ¹/₂ ounce)

¹/₄ cup all-purpose flour

1 teaspoon salt

¹/₂ teaspoon black pepper

1 chicken, cut up (about 5 pounds)

3 tablespoons olive oil

2 ounces pancetta or bacon, chopped

1 medium onion, chopped

2 carrots, thinly sliced

3 cloves garlic, minced

1 cup chicken broth

1 tablespoon tomato paste

1 cup pitted green Italian olives

GREEK LAMB WITH TZATZIKI SAUCE

MAKES 8 SERVINGS

1. Untie and unroll lamb to lie flat; trim fat.

2. For marinade, mince 4 garlic cloves; place in small bowl. Add mustard, rosemary, 2 teaspoons salt and pepper; whisk in ¼ cup oil. Spread mixture evenly over lamb, coating both sides. Place lamb in large resealable food storage bag. Seal bag; refrigerate at least 2 hours or overnight, turning several times.

3. Meanwhile for tzatziki sauce, mince 4 garlic cloves and mash to a paste; place in medium bowl. Peel and grate cucumber; squeeze to remove excess moisture. Add cucumber, mint, 2 teaspoons oil and lemon juice to bowl with garlic. Add yogurt; mix well. Season to taste with salt. Refrigerate until ready to serve.

4. Prepare grill for direct cooking. Grill lamb over medium-high heat 35 to 40 minutes or to desired doneness. Cover loosely with foil; let rest 5 to 10 minutes. (Remove from grill at 140°F for medium. Temperature will rise 5°F while resting.)

5. Slice lamb and serve with tzatziki sauce.

NOTE: Lamb can be roasted in the oven instead of grilled. Preheat oven to 325°F. Place lamb on rack in roasting pan. Roast about 1½ hours or to desired doneness. Cover loosely with foil; let rest 5 to 10 minutes. (Remove from oven at 140°F for medium. Temperature will rise 5°F while resting.)

LAMB

- 2½ to 3 pounds boneless leg of lamb
- 4 cloves garlic
- ¼ cup Dijon mustard
- 2 tablespoons minced fresh rosemary leaves
- 2 teaspoons salt
- 2 teaspoons black pepper
- ¼ cup olive oil

TZATZIKI SAUCE

- 4 cloves garlic
- 1 small English cucumber
- 1 tablespoon chopped fresh mint
- 2 teaspoons olive oil
- 1 teaspoon lemon juice
- 2 cups plain Greek yogurt or other thick plain yogurt
- Salt

CHICKEN AND COUSCOUS WITH PISTACHIOS

MAKES 4 SERVINGS

1. Combine allspice, cinnamon, black pepper, ginger, mustard, cloves, red pepper and coriander in small bowl. Sprinkle chicken with 1 teaspoon spice mixture and salt.

2. Heat oil in large nonstick skillet over medium-high heat. Add chicken; cook without stirring 1½ minutes or until golden. Turn chicken; cook 1½ minutes until no longer pink in center.

3. Add broth; bring to a boil. Add couscous and ½ teaspoon spice mixture; cook 1 minute. Stir in raisins, pistachios, parsley and lemon peel; cover and let stand 5 minutes. Fluff with fork before serving.

NOTE: Couscous looks like a grain but, like pasta, it is actually made from semolina flour. It is a staple of North African cuisine where it is often served alongside slow-cooked meat and vegetables.

¾ teaspoon ground allspice

½ teaspoon ground cinnamon

½ teaspoon black pepper

¼ teaspoon ground ginger

¼ teaspoon ground mustard

⅛ teaspoon ground cloves

⅛ teaspoon ground red pepper

⅛ teaspoon ground coriander

12 ounces boneless skinless chicken breasts, cut into 1-inch pieces

½ teaspoon salt

1 tablespoon olive oil

1 can (about 14 ounces) chicken broth

1 cup uncooked couscous

¼ cup golden raisins

¼ cup pistachios

¼ cup chopped fresh parsley

1 teaspoon grated lemon peel

FISH & SEAFOOD

LEMON-GARLIC SALMON WITH TZATZIKI SAUCE

MAKES 4 SERVINGS

1. Place cucumber in small colander set over small bowl; sprinkle with ¼ teaspoon salt. Drain 1 hour.

2. For tzatziki sauce, stir yogurt, cucumber, 1 tablespoon lemon juice, ½ teaspoon lemon peel, ½ teaspoon garlic and ¼ teaspoon salt in small bowl. Cover and refrigerate until ready to serve.

3. Combine remaining 1 tablespoon lemon juice, ½ teaspoon lemon peel, ½ teaspoon garlic, ¼ teaspoon salt and pepper in small bowl; mix well. Rub evenly all over salmon.

4. Heat nonstick grill pan over medium-high heat. Cook salmon 5 minutes per side or until fish begins to flake when tested with fork. Serve with tzatziki sauce.

½ cup diced cucumber

¾ teaspoon salt, divided

1 cup plain Greek yogurt

2 tablespoons fresh lemon juice, divided

1 teaspoon grated lemon peel, divided

1 teaspoon minced garlic, divided

¼ teaspoon black pepper

4 skinless salmon fillets (4 ounces each)

PESTO PASTA WITH SCALLOPS

MAKES 4 SERVINGS

1. Prepare pasta according to package directions in large saucepan of boiling salted water until al dente. Drain, reserving ½ cup cooking water; return to saucepan and keep warm.

2. Meanwhile, heat 2 teaspoons oil in medium skillet over medium heat. Add asparagus; cook 5 minutes, stirring occasionally. Add tomatoes, ¼ teaspoon salt and ¼ teaspoon black pepper, cover and cook over low heat about 5 minutes, stirring occasionally. Add to pasta; cover to keep warm.

3. Combine scallops, 1 teaspoon oil, lemon juice, garlic and remaining ¼ teaspoon black pepper in large bowl; toss to coat.

4. Heat remaining 1 tablespoon oil in same skillet over medium-high heat. Add scallops and remaining ¼ teaspoon salt; cook about 3 minutes per side or until scallops are opaque.

5. Stir pesto and red pepper flakes, if desired, into pasta mixture. Stir in some of reserved pasta water to make a creamy sauce. Divide pasta mixture among serving bowls; top with scallops.

PESTO: Place 1 cup tightly packed fresh basil leaves, ¼ cup pine nuts, 2 cloves garlic and ¼ teaspoon salt in food processor. With motor running, add ¼ cup olive oil in thin steady stream; process until well blended and pine nuts are finely chopped. Add ¼ cup grated Parmesan cheese; pulse until blended.

8 ounces uncooked whole wheat rotini

6 teaspoons olive oil, divided

12 ounces asparagus (about 20 spears), cut into 2-inch-pieces

8 ounces cherry tomatoes, halved (about 2 cups)

½ teaspoon salt, divided

½ teaspoon black pepper, divided

12 ounces large sea scallops

1 tablespoon lemon juice

1 clove garlic, crushed

½ cup homemade or store-bought pesto (recipe follows)

Pinch red pepper flakes (optional)

SHRIMP SCAMPI
MAKES 4 TO 6 SERVINGS

1. Heat butter in large skillet over medium heat. Add garlic; cook and stir 1 to 2 minutes or until softened but not browned. Add shrimp, green onions, wine and lemon juice; cook 2 to 4 minutes or until shrimp are pink and opaque, stirring occasionally.

2. Sprinkle with parsley; season with salt and pepper. Serve with lemon wedges, if desired.

NOTE: Clarifying butter is a process that separates milk solids from the butterfat, producing a cooking fat with a high smoke point, making it perfect for sautéeing. To clarify butter, melt butter in small saucepan over low heat. Skim off white foam that forms on top, then strain remaining butter through cheesecloth. Discard cheesecloth and milky residue in bottom of pan. Clarified butter can be stored in airtight container in refrigerator up to 2 months.

1/3 cup clarified butter

2 to 4 tablespoons minced garlic

1 1/2 pounds large raw shrimp, peeled and deveined

6 green onions, thinly sliced

1/4 cup dry white wine

2 tablespoons lemon juice

Chopped fresh Italian parsley

Salt and black pepper

Lemon wedges (optional)

ROASTED SALMON WITH LENTILS AND SQUASH

MAKES 4 SERVINGS

1. Preheat oven to 400°F. Line shallow baking pan with foil. Spray foil with nonstick cooking spray.

2. Combine lentils, 2 cups water and $1/2$ teaspoon salt in medium saucepan. Bring to a boil. Reduce heat; simmer 15 to 18 minutes or until lentils are just tender but not mushy. Drain.

3. Meanwhile, combine pesto, lemon peel and lemon juice in small bowl; mix well. Set aside.

4. Sprinkle salmon with remaining $1/2$ teaspoon salt and $1/8$ teaspoon black pepper. Place in prepared baking pan. Bake 10 minutes or until fish just begins to flake when tested with fork.

5. Heat oil in large nonstick skillet over medium heat. Add bell pepper and onion; cook and stir 3 minutes. Add squash; cook about 5 minutes or until crisp-tender, stirring frequently. Stir in lentils, $1/4$ cup pesto mixture and remaining $1/8$ teaspoon black pepper. Divide vegetable mixture evenly among four serving plates.

6. Cut salmon into four pieces; place on vegetable mixture. Spread remaining pesto mixture over salmon.

$3/4$ cup dried brown lentils, rinsed and sorted

2 cups water

1 teaspoon salt, divided

$1/2$ cup homemade or store-bought pesto (page 138)

1 teaspoon grated lemon peel

$1/4$ cup fresh lemon juice

1 pound salmon fillet ($1^1/2$ inches thick)

$1/4$ teaspoon black pepper, divided

1 tablespoon olive oil

1 medium red bell pepper, thinly sliced

1 small onion, thinly sliced

1 medium yellow summer squash, cut into ribbons with spiralizer, cut with a julienne peeler or thinly sliced

ADRIATIC-STYLE HALIBUT

MAKES 4 SERVINGS

1. Preheat oven to 200°F. Combine tomato, olives and garlic in small bowl; mix well.

2. Season fish with ¾ teaspoon salt and ¼ teaspoon pepper. Heat oil in large nonstick skillet over medium heat. Add fish; cook 8 to 10 minutes or just until fish is opaque in center, turning once. Transfer to serving platter; keep warm in oven.

3. Add wine to skillet; cook over high heat until reduced by half. Add tomato mixture; cook and stir 1 to 2 minutes or until heated through. Season with additional salt and pepper. Spoon tomato mixture over fish; sprinkle with basil.

1 large tomato, seeded and diced

⅓ cup sliced pitted kalamata olives

1 clove garlic, minced

4 skinless halibut or red snapper fillets (about 6 ounces each)

¾ teaspoon coarse salt

¼ teaspoon black pepper

1 tablespoon olive oil

¼ cup dry white wine or vermouth

2 tablespoons chopped fresh basil or Italian parsley

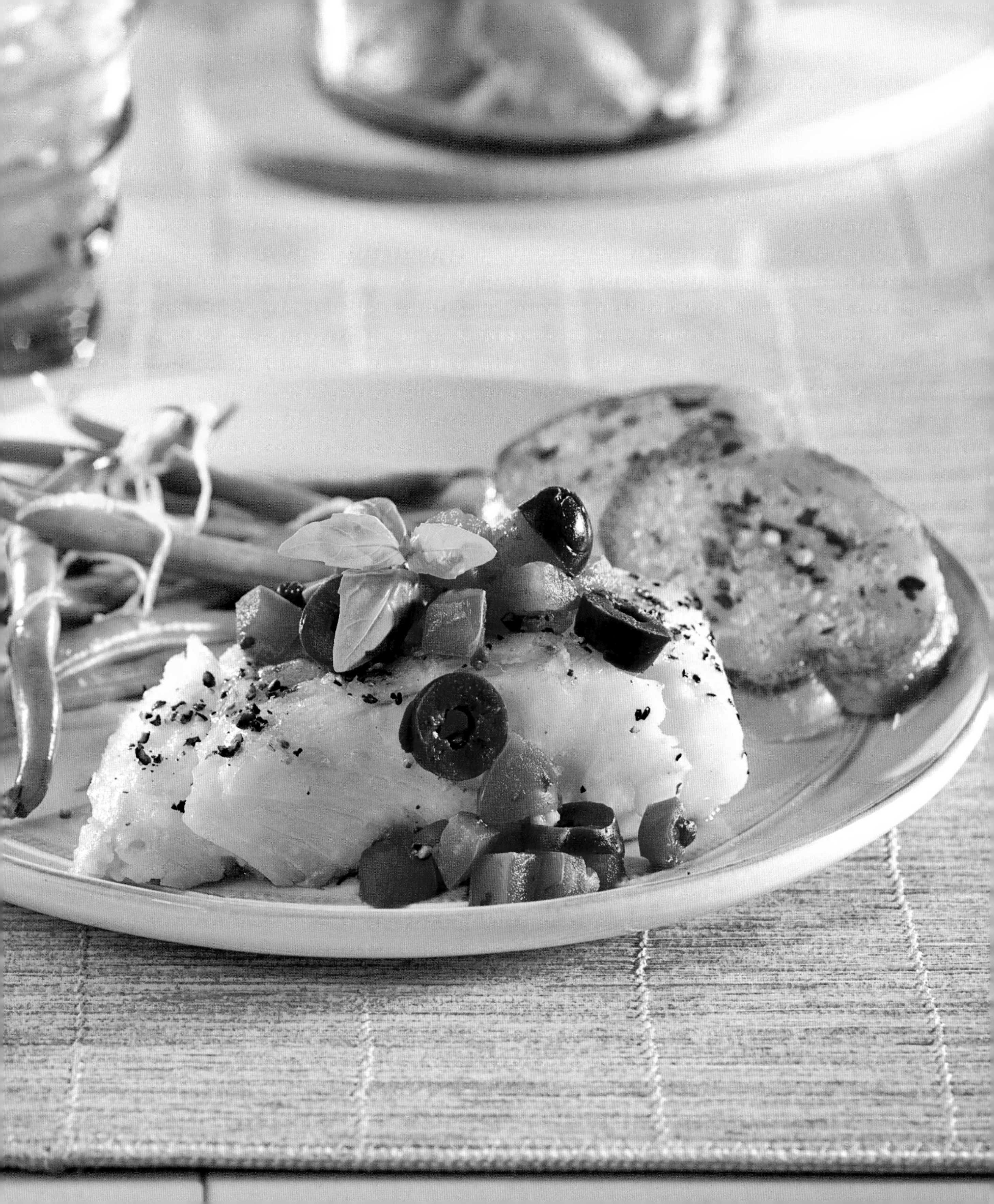

SEARED SCALLOPS OVER GARLIC-LEMON SPINACH

MAKES 4 SERVINGS

1. Heat oil in large nonstick skillet over medium-high heat. Add scallops; sprinkle with salt and pepper. Cook 2 to 3 minutes per side or until golden. Transfer to large plate; keep warm.

2. Add shallot and garlic to skillet; cook and stir 45 seconds or until fragrant. Add spinach; cook 2 minutes or until spinach just begins to wilt, stirring occasionally. Remove from heat; stir in lemon juice.

3. Serve scallops over spinach. Garnish with lemon wedges.

1 tablespoon olive oil

1 pound sea scallops* (approximately 12)

$\frac{1}{4}$ teaspoon salt

$\frac{1}{8}$ teaspoon black pepper

1 shallot, minced

2 cloves garlic, minced

1 package (6 ounces) baby spinach

1 tablespoon fresh lemon juice

Lemon wedges (optional)

Make sure scallops are dry before putting them in the skillet so they can get a golden crust.

SHRIMP CAPRESE PASTA

MAKES 4 SERVINGS

1. Cook pasta according to package directions in large saucepan of boiling salted water to al dente. Drain, reserving $1/2$ cup cooking water; return to saucepan and keep warm.

2. Heat oil in large skillet over medium heat. Add 2 cups chopped tomatoes, reserved $1/2$ cup pasta water, 2 tablespoons basil, vinegar, garlic, salt and red pepper flakes. Cook and stir 10 minutes or until tomatoes begin to soften.

3. Add shrimp and 1 cup halved tomatoes to skillet; cook and stir 5 minutes or until shrimp turn pink and opaque. Add pasta; cook until heated through.

4. Divide mixture evenly among serving bowls. Top evenly with cheese and remaining 2 tablespoons basil.

1 cup uncooked whole wheat penne

2 teaspoons olive oil

2 cups coarsely chopped grape tomatoes

4 tablespoons chopped fresh basil, divided

1 tablespoon balsamic vinegar

2 cloves garlic, minced

$1/4$ teaspoon salt

$1/8$ teaspoon red pepper flakes

8 ounces medium raw shrimp, peeled and deveined

1 cup grape tomatoes, halved

2 ounces fresh mozzarella pearls

TUNISIAN FISH WITH COUSCOUS

MAKES 6 SERVINGS

1. Heat oil in large saucepan over medium heat. Add onions and garlic; cook and stir 5 minutes or until onions are tender. Stir in tomato paste, cumin, paprika and cinnamon. Cook 1 minute, stirring constantly.

2. Add 5 cups chicken broth. Increase heat to high. Bring mixture to a boil. Reduce heat to low; cover and simmer 10 minutes. Add potatoes; cover and simmer 10 minutes. Add carrots, bell pepper, chickpeas and salt; cover and simmer 5 minutes.

3. Rinse fish fillets; pat dry with paper towels. Cut into 2×1-inch strips. Add fish to saucepan; cover and simmer 5 to 7 minutes until fish flakes easily when tested with fork.

4. Bring remaining 3 cups broth to a boil in medium saucepan over medium-high heat. Stir in couscous. Remove from heat. Cover; let stand 5 minutes or until liquid is absorbed. Fluff with fork.

5. Spoon couscous into shallow bowls; top with fish and vegetables.

- ¼ cup olive oil
- 2 cups chopped onions
- 8 cloves garlic, minced
- 2 tablespoons tomato paste
- 1 tablespoon ground cumin
- 1 tablespoon paprika
- ½ teaspoon ground cinnamon
- 8 cups chicken broth, divided
- 1½ pounds small potatoes, quartered
- 5 medium carrots, peeled and cut into 2×¼-inch strips
- 1 red bell pepper, seeded and cut into ½-inch strips
- 1 can (about 15 ounces) chickpeas, rinsed and drained
- ½ teaspoon salt
- 6 grouper fillets (about 5 ounces each)
- 2 cups uncooked whole wheat or regular couscous

SHRIMP, GOAT CHEESE AND LEEK TORTILLA

MAKES 6 SERVINGS

1. Preheat oven to 350°F. Cut each shrimp into 4 pieces.

2. Heat 2 tablespoons oil in medium ovenproof skillet over medium-high heat. Add garlic; cook and stir 30 seconds or just until fragrant. Add shrimp; cook and stir 3 to 4 minutes or until shrimp are pink and opaque. Transfer to plate.

3. Heat remaining 2 tablespoons oil in same skillet over medium heat. Add leeks; cook and stir 4 to 5 minutes or until tender. Place on plate with shrimp; cool 5 minutes.

4. Whisk eggs in medium bowl; season with salt and pepper. Crumble goat cheese into eggs. Stir in shrimp and leeks.

5. Heat same skillet over medium-low heat. Add egg mixture; cook 5 minutes or until edge begins to set. Transfer skillet to oven; bake 10 to 12 minutes or until surface is puffy and center is just set. Cool 10 minutes. Cut into wedges; serve warm or at room temperature.

8 ounces medium raw shrimp, peeled and deveined

4 tablespoons olive oil, divided

2 cloves garlic, minced

2 leeks, chopped

7 eggs

Salt and black pepper

1 package (3 ounces) goat cheese

BREADS

SAVORY PITA CHIPS

MAKES 4 SERVINGS

1. Preheat oven to 350°F. Line baking sheet with foil.

2. Carefully cut each pita round in half horizontally; split into two rounds. Cut each round into 6 wedges.

3. Place wedges in large bowl. Add oil; stir until coated. Place in single layer on prepared baking sheet.

4. Combine Parmesan, basil and garlic powder in small bowl; sprinkle evenly over pita wedges.

5. Bake 12 to 14 minutes or until golden brown. Cool completely.

2 whole wheat or white pita bread rounds

2 tablespoons olive oil

3 tablespoons grated Parmesan cheese

1 teaspoon dried basil

¼ teaspoon garlic powder

PITA BREAD
MAKES 8 PITA BREADS

1. Combine flour, salt, sugar and yeast in large bowl; whisk until well blended. Add water and oil; stir with wooden spoon until rough dough forms. If dough appears too dry, add additional 1 to 2 tablespoons water. Attach dough hook to stand mixer; knead on low speed 5 minutes. Grease large bowl with olive oil or nonstick cooking spray. Place dough in bowl; turn to grease top. Cover with plastic wrap; let rise in warm place 1 hour or until doubled in size.

2. Preheat oven to 500°F. Turn out dough onto work surface; press into circle. Cut dough into 8 wedges. Roll each wedge into a smooth ball; flatten slightly. Let stand 10 minutes for gluten to relax. Roll each ball into circle about 1/4 inch thick. Place circles on two ungreased baking sheets.

3. Bake one baking sheet at a time 5 minutes or until pitas are puffed and set. Cool on wire rack.

3½ cups all-purpose flour

1 tablespoon salt

1 tablespoon sugar

1 package (¼ ounce) rapid-rise active dry yeast (2¼ teaspoons)

1½ cups warm water (120°F)

2 tablespoons olive oil

WALNUT FIG BREAD

MAKES 1 LOAF

1. Combine 1 cup all-purpose flour, whole wheat flour, yeast, fennel seeds and salt in large bowl. Combine water, oil and honey in small saucepan; heat to 120°F. Add to flour mixture; stir until moistened. Add egg; stir until smooth. Add enough remaining all-purpose flour to form soft dough. Stir in figs and walnuts.

2. Turn dough out onto lightly floured surface; knead 5 to 6 minutes or until smooth and elastic, or knead with dough hook of electric mixer on low speed 5 to 7 minutes. Shape dough into a ball. Place in large greased bowl; turn to grease top. Cover and let rise in warm place 1 hour or until doubled in size.

3. Punch dough down. Shape into round loaf; place on greased baking sheet. Cover and let rise in warm place 40 minutes.

4. Preheat oven to 350°F. Bake 30 to 35 minutes or until browned. Cool on wire rack.

2¼ cups all-purpose flour, divided

1 cup whole wheat flour

1 package (¼ ounce) rapid-rise active dry yeast (2¼ teaspoons)

1 tablespoon whole fennel seeds

1½ teaspoons salt

1 cup water

2 tablespoons olive oil

1 tablespoon honey

1 egg

1 cup chopped dried figs

½ cup chopped walnuts, toasted*

To toast walnuts, spread in single layer in heavy skillet. Cook over medium heat 2 to 3 minutes or until lightly browned, stirring frequently.

SOCCA (FARINATA)

MAKES 6 SERVINGS

1. Sift chickpea flour into medium bowl. Stir in salt and pepper. Gradually whisk in water until smooth. Stir in 2 tablespoons oil. Let stand at least 30 minutes.

2. Preheat oven to 450°F. Place 9- or 10-inch cast iron skillet in oven to heat.

3. Add basil, rosemary and thyme to batter; whisk until smooth. Carefully remove skillet from oven. Add 2 tablespoons oil to skillet, swirling to coat pan evenly. Immediately pour in batter.

4. Bake 12 to 15 minutes or until edge of pancake begins to pull away from side of pan and center is firm. Remove from oven. Preheat broiler.

5. Brush with remaining 1 tablespoon oil. Broil 2 to 4 minutes or until dark brown in spots. Cut into wedges. Serve warm.

NOTE: Socca are pancakes made of chickpea flour and are commonly served in paper cones as a savory street food in the south of France, especially around Nice. To make a thinner, softer crêpe, just increase the amount of water in the recipe by about 1/4 cup and cook in batches in a skillet.

1 cup chickpea flour

3/4 teaspoon salt

1/2 teaspoon black pepper

1 cup water

5 tablespoons olive oil, divided

1 1/2 teaspoons minced fresh basil *or* 1/2 teaspoon dried basil

1 teaspoon minced fresh rosemary *or* 1/4 teaspoon dried rosemary

1/4 teaspoon dried thyme

RED PEPPER, ROSEMARY AND PANCETTA FLATBREAD

MAKES 6 SERVINGS

1. Prepare basic pizza dough. Preheat oven to 400°F. Roll out pizza dough into 15×10-inch rectangle on lightly floured surface. Place on sheet pan. Fold edges over to form ¹/₂-inch rim. Bake 5 minutes.

2. Heat oil in large skillet over medium heat. Add onion and salt; cook and stir 5 minutes or until softened. Add pancetta, sun-dried tomatoes and garlic; cook and stir 4 minutes. Spread over crust; top with peppers, rosemary and cheese.

3. Bake 10 minutes or until cheese melts and crust edges are brown.

NOTE: Pancetta is Italian bacon. Unlike American bacon, which is most often smoked, pancetta is unsmoked pork belly has been cured in salt and spices such as nutmeg, black pepper and fennel and then dried for a few months.

Basic Pizza Dough (recipe follows)

- 2 tablespoons olive oil
- 1 large yellow onion, thinly sliced
- ¹/₂ teaspoon salt
- 2 ounces pancetta, chopped
- 2 tablespoons minced sun-dried tomatoes
- 2 cloves garlic, minced
- 1 jar (7 ounces) roasted red peppers, drained and sliced
- 1 tablespoon chopped fresh rosemary
- ¹/₂ cup shredded Parmesan cheese

BASIC PIZZA DOUGH

1. Combine flour, yeast and salt in large bowl of stand mixer. Stir in water and oil to form rough dough. Knead with dough hook on low speed 5 to 7 minutes or until dough is smooth and elastic.

2. Shape dough into a ball. Place in greased bowl; turn to grease top. Cover and let rise in warm place about 45 minutes or until doubled in size. Punch down dough.

3. Use immediately or shape into a ball, wrap in plastic wrap and refrigerate until ready to use.

3 cups all-purpose flour

1 package (¼ ounce) rapid-rise active dry yeast (2¼ teaspoons)

1 teaspoon salt

1 cup warm water (120°F)

2 tablespoons olive oil

GANNAT (FRENCH CHEESE BREAD)

MAKES 1 LOAF

1. Combine 3 tablespoons water, yeast and sugar in small bowl. Stir to dissolve yeast; let stand 5 minutes or until bubbly.

2. Place flour, butter and salt in food processor or blender; process 15 seconds or until mixed. Add yeast mixture and eggs; process 15 seconds or until blended.

3. With motor running, drizzle in just enough remaining water in thin stream until dough forms a ball that cleans the sides of the bowl. Process until ball turns around bowl about 25 times. Turn off processor and let dough stand 1 to 2 minutes.

4. Turn on processor and gradually drizzle in enough remaining water to make dough soft, smooth and satiny but not sticky. Process until dough turns around bowl about 15 times.

5. Turn dough onto lightly floured surface; shape into a ball. Place in lightly greased bowl; turn to grease top. Cover and let rise in warm place 1 hour or until doubled in size.

6. Grease 9-inch round cake pan with 1 teaspoon oil. Punch down dough. Place dough on lightly greased surface; knead cheese into dough. Roll or pat into 8-inch circle. Place in prepared pan; brush with remaining 1 teaspoon oil. Cover and let rise in warm place about 45 minutes or until doubled in size.

7. Preheat oven to 375°F. Bake 30 to 35 minutes or until browned and bread sounds hollow when tapped. Immediately remove from pan; cool on wire rack.

3 to 6 tablespoons warm water (105° to 115°F)

1 package (¼ ounce) rapid-rise active dry yeast (2¼ teaspoons)

1 teaspoon sugar

2½ cups all-purpose flour

¼ cup (½ stick) butter, at room temperature

1 teaspoon salt

2 eggs

2 teaspoons olive oil, divided

4 ounces Emmentaler Swiss, Gruyère or Swiss cheese, shredded

WILD MUSHROOM FLATBREAD

MAKES 8 SERVINGS

1. Prepare basic pizza dough. Preheat oven to 400°F. Line baking sheet with parchment paper or spray with nonstick cooking spray.

2. Roll out dough on lightly floured surface into 15×10-inch rectangle. Place on prepared baking sheet. Bake 10 minutes.

3. Meanwhile, heat oil in large skillet over medium-high heat. Add mushrooms; cook and stir 5 minutes. Add shallot and garlic; cook and stir 5 minutes or until tender. Season with salt.

4. Spread mushroom mixture evenly over prepared pizza crust. Top with cheese and thyme.

5. Bake 8 minutes or until cheese is melted. Cut into squares to serve.

Basic Pizza Dough (recipe page 163)

2 teaspoons olive oil

1 package (4 ounces) sliced cremini mushrooms

1 package (4 ounces) sliced shiitake mushrooms

1 shallot, thinly sliced

2 cloves garlic, minced

1/2 teaspoon salt

3/4 cup (3 ounces) shredded Gruyère cheese

2 teaspoons chopped fresh thyme

HONEY-PECAN TWIST

MAKES 1 LOAF

1. Heat milk, oil and 3 tablespoons honey in small saucepan over low heat until warm (120°F). Combine 2¼ cups flour, yeast and salt in large bowl of stand mixer. Add milk mixture and 2 eggs; beat on medium-low speed 2 minutes or until well blended. Gradually add enough additional flour until rough dough forms.

2. Attach dough hook to mixer; knead on low speed 5 to 7 minutes or until dough is smooth and elastic, adding additional flour by tablespoons if needed. Shape dough into a ball. Place in large greased bowl; turn to grease top. Cover and let rise in warm place 35 to 40 minutes or until dough has increased in size by one third. Punch down dough; turn out onto lightly floured surface. Roll out into 14×8-inch rectangle using lightly floured rolling pin.

3. Combine 1 cup pecans, brown sugar, butter, cinnamon and 3 tablespoons honey in small bowl. Spread evenly over dough; press in gently with fingertips. Starting from one long end, roll up tightly, jelly-roll style. Pinch seams lightly; turn seam side down. Flatten slightly. Twist dough 6 to 8 turns. Grease 9-inch cake pan. Place dough in pan in a loose spiral starting in center and working to the side. Tuck outside end under dough; pinch to seal. Loosely cover with lightly greased sheet of plastic wrap. Let rise in warm place 1 hour or until doubled in size.

4. Preheat oven to 350°F. Place pan on baking sheet. Beat remaining egg with 1 teaspoon water in small bowl; brush all over dough. Drizzle remaining 3 tablespoons honey evenly over top; sprinkle with remaining ¼ cup pecans. Bake about 45 minutes or until deep golden brown. Turn pan and tent with sheet of foil halfway through baking time to prevent burning. Remove foil for last 5 minutes of baking. Cool in pan on wire rack 5 minutes. Remove from pan. Cool completely on wire rack.

⅔ cup milk

6 tablespoons olive oil

9 tablespoons honey, divided

2½ to 3½ cups all-purpose flour, divided

1 package (¼ ounce) rapid-rise active dry yeast (2¼ teaspoons)

¾ teaspoon salt

3 eggs, divided

1¼ cups coarsely chopped pecans, toasted,* divided

3 tablespoons packed brown sugar

1½ tablespoons butter, melted

1 tablespoon ground cinnamon

1 teaspoon water

FOCACCIA

MAKES 12 SERVINGS

1. Sprinkle yeast and sugar over warm water in large bowl; stir until dissolved. Let stand 5 minutes or until mixture is bubbly. Add 3½ cups flour, 3 tablespoons oil and salt; stir until soft dough forms.

2. Turn out dough onto lightly floured surface. Knead 5 minutes or until smooth and elastic, gradually adding remaining flour to prevent sticking, if necessary. Or use stand mixer with dough hook attachment; knead on low speed 5 minutes. Shape dough into a ball. Place in large greased bowl; turn to grease top. Cover and let rise in warm place 1 hour or until doubled in size.

3. Brush sheet pan with 1 tablespoon oil. Punch down dough. Turn out dough onto lightly floured surface. Flatten into rectangle; roll out almost to size of pan. Transfer dough to pan; gently press to edges of pan. Poke surface of dough all over with fingers, making indentations every 1 or 2 inches. Brush with remaining 3 tablespoons oil. Gently press peppers and olives into dough. Cover and let rise in warm place 30 minutes or until doubled in size. Preheat oven to 450°F.

4. Bake 12 to 18 minutes or until golden brown. Cut into squares or rectangles. Serve warm.

1 package (¼ ounce) rapid-rise active dry yeast (2¼ teaspoons)

1 teaspoon sugar

1½ cups warm water (105° to 110°F)

4 cups all-purpose flour, divided

7 tablespoons olive oil, divided

1 teaspoon salt

¼ cup bottled roasted red peppers, drained and cut into strips

¼ cup pitted black olives

CHERRY-ALMOND CLAFOUTIS

MAKES 4 SERVINGS

1. Preheat oven to 350°F. Spray 4 (6-ounce) ramekins with nonstick cooking spray; place on baking sheet.

2. Process almonds in food processor until coarsely ground. Add powdered sugar; pulse until well blended. Add flour, granulated sugar and salt. Pulse until well blended. Gradually add butter through feed tube, pulsing just until blended.

3. Combine milk, eggs and vanilla in small bowl. With motor running, gradually add milk mixture to almond mixture. Process until blended. Remove blade from food processor; gently stir in cherries.

4. Divide batter among prepared ramekins. Bake about 50 minutes or until tops and sides are puffy and golden. Let cool 5 to 10 minutes.

NOTE: Clafoutis is a traditional French dessert made by layering a sweet batter over fresh fruit. The result is a rich dessert with a cake-like topping and a pudding-like center.

½ cup slivered almonds, toasted*

½ cup powdered sugar

⅔ cup all-purpose flour

⅔ cup granulated sugar

¼ teaspoon salt

½ cup (1 stick) cold butter, cut into pieces

⅔ cup milk

2 eggs

½ teaspoon vanilla

1 cup fresh cherries, pitted and quartered or raspberries

To toast almonds, spread in single layer on baking sheet. Bake in preheated 350°F oven 8 to 10 minutes or until golden brown, stirring frequently.

BAKLAVA
MAKES ABOUT 32 PIECES

1. Place half of walnuts in food processor. Pulse until nuts are finely chopped, but not pasty. Transfer to large bowl; repeat with remaining nuts. Add $1/2$ cup sugar, ground cinnamon, salt and ground cloves; mix well.

2. Preheat oven to 325°F. Brush 13×9-inch baking dish with some of melted butter or line with foil, leaving overhang on two sides for easy removal. Unroll phyllo dough and place on large sheet of waxed paper. Trim phyllo sheets to 13×9 inches. Cover phyllo with plastic wrap and damp, clean kitchen towel to prevent drying out.

3. Place 1 phyllo sheet in bottom of dish, folding in edges if too long; brush with butter. Repeat with 7 additional phyllo sheets, brushing each sheet with butter as it is layered. Sprinkle about $1/2$ cup nut mixture evenly over layered phyllo. Top nuts with 3 additional layers of phyllo, brushing each sheet with butter. Sprinkle with $1/2$ cup nut mixture. Repeat layering and brushing of 3 phyllo sheets with $1/2$ cup nut mixture two more times. Top final layer of nut mixture with remaining phyllo sheets, brushing each sheet with butter.

4. Score baklava lengthwise into 4 equal sections, then cut diagonally at $1^{1}/_{2}$-inch intervals to form diamond shapes. Sprinkle top lightly with water to prevent top phyllo layers from curling up during baking. Bake 50 to 60 minutes or until golden brown.

5. Meanwhile, combine $1^{1}/_{2}$ cups water, remaining $3/4$ cup sugar, honey, lemon peel, lemon juice, cinnamon stick and whole cloves in medium saucepan; bring to a boil over high heat. Reduce heat to low; simmer 15 minutes. Strain hot syrup; drizzle evenly over hot baklava. Cool completely in baking dish on wire rack. Cut into pieces along score lines.

4 cups walnuts, shelled pistachios and/or slivered almonds (1 pound)

$1^{1}/_{4}$ cups sugar, divided

2 teaspoons ground cinnamon

$1/4$ teaspoon salt

$1/4$ teaspoon ground cloves

1 cup (2 sticks) butter, melted

1 package (16 ounces) frozen phyllo dough (about 20 sheets), thawed

$1^{1}/_{2}$ cups water

$3/4$ cup honey

2 (2-inch-long) strips lemon peel

1 tablespoon fresh lemon juice

1 cinnamon stick

3 whole cloves

CITRUS OLIVE OIL CAKE

MAKES 8 TO 10 SERVINGS

1. Preheat oven to 350°F. Spray 9-inch round cake pan with nonstick cooking spray. Line bottom of pan with parchment paper; spray paper.

2. Whisk flour, sugar, salt, baking soda and baking powder in large bowl.

3. Whisk oil, buttermilk, eggs, orange peel, orange juice, lemon peel and lemon juice in medium bowl. Add to dry ingredients; whisk just until blended. Pour batter into prepared pan.

4. Bake 40 minutes or until the top is golden and toothpick inserted into center comes out clean. Cool completely in pan on wire rack. Invert onto serving plate.

5. Meanwhile, combine $3/4$ cup orange juice and 2 tablespoons sugar in small saucepan; bring to a boil over medium-high heat. Reduce heat to medium; cook 10 to 12 minutes or until mixture thickens and is reduced to about $1/4$ cup. Cool slightly.

6. Pour syrup over cake; cool completely before serving. Garnish with additional orange peel and mint leaves.

CAKE

$1^3/4$ cups all-purpose flour

$1^1/2$ cups sugar

1 teaspoon salt

$1/2$ teaspoon baking soda

$1/2$ teaspoon baking powder

1 cup extra virgin olive oil

1 cup buttermilk

3 eggs

Grated peel and juice of 1 orange

Grated peel and juice of 1 lemon

ORANGE SYRUP

$3/4$ cup orange juice

2 tablespoons sugar

GRILLED PEACHES WITH NUTMEG PASTRY CREAM

MAKES 4 SERVINGS

1. Prepare grill for direct cooking. Combine 2 tablespoons sugar and cinnamon in small bowl; sprinkle over peach halves. Grill peaches over medium-low heat just until tender and slightly golden brown. (Peaches should still be firm and hold shape.) Set aside.

2. Combine egg yolks, remaining $1/3$ cup sugar, flour and salt in medium bowl; stir until well blended.

3. Bring milk, vanilla and nutmeg to a boil in medium saucepan over medium-low heat. Whisking constantly, slowly add $1/4$ cup hot milk mixture to egg yolk mixture.

4. Add egg yolk mixture to milk mixture in saucepan; cook, whisking constantly, until thickened. Remove from heat and add butter; whisk until well blended.

5. Spoon sauce onto plates; arrange peach halves on top of sauce. Serve with whipped cream, if desired.

$1/3$ cup plus 2 tablespoons sugar, divided

1 teaspoon ground cinnamon

4 peaches, halved

3 egg yolks

2 tablespoons all-purpose flour

Pinch salt

$1^{1}/_{4}$ cups whole milk

1 teaspoon vanilla

$1/8$ teaspoon ground nutmeg

2 tablespoons butter

Whipped cream (optional)

FIGS POACHED IN RED WINE

MAKES 4 SERVINGS

1. Stir together wine, brown sugar, cinnamon sticks, orange peel and figs in medium saucepan. Bring to a simmer over medium heat. Reduce heat to medium-low; cover and simmer 30 minutes or until figs are tender.

2. Transfer figs to bowl with slotted spoon. Increase heat to medium; cook until syrup is thickened and slightly reduced. Stir some of syrup into figs.

3. Place figs on serving plates; drizzle with syrup. Top with spoonful of cream.

2 cups dry red wine

1 cup packed brown sugar

2 (3-inch) cinnamon sticks

1 teaspoon finely grated orange peel

12 dried Calimyrna or Mediterranean figs (about 6 ounces)

4 tablespoons whipping cream or Greek yogurt

GLAZED PLUM PASTRY

MAKES 12 TO 18 SERVINGS

1. Preheat oven to 400°F. Line 18×12-inch baking sheet with parchment paper. Combine 2 tablespoons sugar and flour in small bowl.

2. Unfold pastry sheets on prepared baking sheet. Place pastry sheets side by side so fold lines are parallel to length of baking sheet. Arrange sheets so they overlap $1/2$ inch in center. Press center seam firmly to seal. Trim ends so pastry fits on baking sheet. Prick entire surface of pastry with fork.

3. Sprinkle flour mixture evenly over pastry to within $1/2$ inch of edges. Bake 12 to 15 minutes or until pastry is slightly puffed and golden.

4. Cut plums in half lengthwise; remove pits. Cut crosswise into $1/8$-inch-thick slices. Arrange slices slightly overlapping in 5 rows down length of pastry. Combine remaining 1 tablespoon sugar and cinnamon in small bowl; sprinkle evenly over plums.

5. Bake 15 minutes or until plums are tender and pastry is browned. Remove to wire rack.

6. Microwave preserves in small microwavable bowl on HIGH 30 to 40 seconds or until melted. Brush preserves over plums. Cool 10 to 15 minutes before serving.

3 tablespoons sugar, divided

2 tablespoons all-purpose flour

1 package (about 17 ounces) frozen puff pastry sheets, thawed

8 plums (about 2 pounds)

$1/4$ teaspoon ground cinnamon

$1/3$ cup apricot preserves

COCONUT ALMOND BISCOTTI

MAKES 2 DOZEN BISCOTTI

1. Preheat oven to 350°F. Line baking sheet with parchment paper.

2. Combine flour, coconut, almonds, sugar, baking powder and salt in large bowl.

3. Whisk eggs, butter and vanilla in medium bowl. Add to dry ingredients; mix until blended.

4. Divide dough into two equal pieces. Shape each piece of dough into 8×2¾-inch loaf with lightly floured hands. Place loaves 3 inches apart on prepared baking sheet.

5. Bake loaves 26 to 28 minutes or until golden and set. Cool on wire rack 10 minutes. Using serrated knife, slice each loaf diagonally into ½-inch-thick slices. Place slices, cut sides down, on baking sheet. Bake 20 minutes or until firm and golden. Cool completely on wire rack.

2½ cups all-purpose flour

1⅓ cups unsweetened shredded coconut

¾ cup sliced almonds

⅔ cup sugar

2 teaspoons baking powder

½ teaspoon salt

2 eggs

½ cup (1 stick) butter, melted

1 teaspoon vanilla

ORANGE GRANITA

MAKES 6 SERVINGS

1. Cut oranges in half; squeeze juice into medium bowl and reserve empty shells. Strain juice to remove seeds if necessary.

2. Combine sugar and water in small saucepan; cook over medium heat until sugar is dissolved, stirring frequently. Stir sugar mixture and cinnamon into juice.

3. Pour juice mixture into shallow 9-inch pan. Cover and place on flat surface in freezer. After 1 to 2 hours when ice crystals form at edges, stir with fork. Stir 2 or 3 more times at 20 to 30 minute intervals until texture of granita is like icy snow.

4. Scoop granita into orange shells to serve.

6 small Valencia or blood oranges

$\frac{1}{4}$ cup sugar

$\frac{1}{4}$ cup water

$\frac{1}{8}$ teaspoon ground cinnamon

METRIC CONVERSION CHART

VOLUME MEASUREMENTS (dry)

$\frac{1}{8}$ teaspoon = 0.5 mL
$\frac{1}{4}$ teaspoon = 1 mL
$\frac{1}{2}$ teaspoon = 2 mL
$\frac{3}{4}$ teaspoon = 4 mL
1 teaspoon = 5 mL
1 tablespoon = 15 mL
2 tablespoons = 30 mL
$\frac{1}{4}$ cup = 60 mL
$\frac{1}{3}$ cup = 75 mL
$\frac{1}{2}$ cup = 125 mL
$\frac{2}{3}$ cup = 150 mL
$\frac{3}{4}$ cup = 175 mL
1 cup = 250 mL
2 cups = 1 pint = 500 mL
3 cups = 750 mL
4 cups = 1 quart = 1 L

VOLUME MEASUREMENTS (fluid)

1 fluid ounce (2 tablespoons) = 30 mL
4 fluid ounces ($\frac{1}{2}$ cup) = 125 mL
8 fluid ounces (1 cup) = 250 mL
12 fluid ounces (1$\frac{1}{2}$ cups) = 375 mL
16 fluid ounces (2 cups) = 500 mL

WEIGHTS (mass)

$\frac{1}{2}$ ounce = 15 g
1 ounce = 30 g
3 ounces = 90 g
4 ounces = 120 g
8 ounces = 225 g
10 ounces = 285 g
12 ounces = 360 g
16 ounces = 1 pound = 450 g

DIMENSIONS

$\frac{1}{16}$ inch = 2 mm
$\frac{1}{8}$ inch = 3 mm
$\frac{1}{4}$ inch = 6 mm
$\frac{1}{2}$ inch = 1.5 cm
$\frac{3}{4}$ inch = 2 cm
1 inch = 2.5 cm

OVEN TEMPERATURES

250°F = 120°C
275°F = 140°C
300°F = 150°C
325°F = 160°C
350°F = 180°C
375°F = 190°C
400°F = 200°C
425°F = 220°C
450°F = 230°C

BAKING PAN SIZES

Utensil	Size in Inches/Quarts	Metric Volume	Size in Centimeters
Baking or Cake Pan (square or rectangular)	8×8×2	2 L	20×20×5
	9×9×2	2.5 L	23×23×5
	12×8×2	3 L	30×20×5
	13×9×2	3.5 L	33×23×5
Loaf Pan	8×4×3	1.5 L	20×10×7
	9×5×3	2 L	23×13×7
Round Layer Cake Pan	8×1½	1.2 L	20×4
	9×1½	1.5 L	23×4
Pie Plate	8×1¼	750 mL	20×3
	9×1¼	1 L	23×3
Baking Dish or Casserole	1 quart	1 L	—
	1½ quart	1.5 L	—
	2 quart	2 L	—